STUDENT COOKBOOK CAMPUS CRAVINGS

a students guide to takeaway at home

BEN WILLIAM

TABLE OF CONTENTS

INTRODUCTION

In the heart of the UK's buzzing campus life, where tradition and modernity dance together, there's a scent that every student knows well. As dusk embraces the day, the alluring smell of takeout often drifts through the air, a signal of solace after hours hunched over books. But now, we're turning a new leaf with "Campus Cravings". This isn't just a guide; it's your personal kitchen confidant, here to walk you through creating the magic of your beloved takeout with your own hands, ingenuity, and a friendly nod to your budget. We're not just talking about cooking; we're talking about a culinary revolution in your very own dorm, where every dish is cheaper than your usual takeout and yet, richer in every possible way.

The Joyful Journey of "Campus Cravings":

"Campus Cravings" goes beyond mere mimicry. It's about embracing the flavors you love, adding your own twist, and whipping up something that's not just healthier, but also gives your taste buds a reason to celebrate.

A Toast to UK's Takeout Gems:

From the crunchy fish and chips on a breezy evening to the warm, spicy curries that fend off the winter chill, takeout is not just food; it's a collection of moments. Now, with a few clicks on our phones, a world of flavors awaits us. But what if we bring that world right into our dorm kitchens?

The Sweet Perks of Going Homemade:

Healthier Choices at Your Fingertips: With "Campus Cravings", you call the shots. Want to slash the calories or go all organic? You're the chef!

Saving Your Coins: Skip the extra costs of takeout. "Campus Cravings" shows you how to whip up meals that are kind to your wallet without skimping on the yum factor.

Tailored to Taste: Fancy a little extra kick or a double dose of cheese? Here's how you can make dishes that cater to exactly what you're craving.

Cooking Up Connections: There's magic in cooking together. "Campus Cravings" is all about transforming meal prep into a memorable, bonding experience with your college mates.

So, are you ready to embark on this flavorsome quest? Flip the page and dive into a collection of recipes that traverse the globe, from nostalgic comforts to new discoveries. Whether you're a kitchen newbie or a seasoned foodie, "Campus Cravings" is set to be your trusty sidekick, promising a journey filled with surprises, joy, and a closer relationship with the food on your plate. Get your apron ready and let's create some takeout wonders together, right here on campus!

Tips and Tricks for Mastering "Campus Cravings" Recipes

Welcome to the practical side of your "Campus Cravings" journey! Cooking can be as much about intuition and improvisation as it is about following recipes. Here's a treasure of tips and tricks to help you navigate through the recipes in this book and make the most out of your campus kitchen.

- **Get to Know Your Spices:** Spices are the soul of any dish. Start with a basic set and learn how they interact. A dash of cumin adds warmth, a sprinkle of paprika brings a smoky zest, and a pinch of turmeric can brighten any dish. Experiment to see what works for you!
- **The Art of Substitution:** Don't have an ingredient? No problem. Learn to substitute where necessary. No sour cream? Use yogurt. Out of fresh herbs? Dried ones will do in a pinch. Embrace flexibility, and you'll become a more resourceful cook.
- **Efficiency is Key:** Read through the entire recipe before you begin. Prep all your ingredients (a technique called mise en place) to streamline your cooking process. This not only saves time but also ensures you're not scrambling while your dish is on the fire.
- **Invest in a Good Knife:** A sharp, comfortable knife can make all the difference. It's a worthy investment that will make prep work quicker, easier, and safer.
- **Master the Basic Techniques:** Skills like chopping onions, cooking pasta to al dente, and making a roux are foundations you can build upon. Once you've nailed these, you can tackle any recipe in this book with confidence.
- **One-Pot Wonders:** Embrace recipes that can be made in a single pot or pan. These tend to be easy, require less clean-up, and are perfect for a busy student life. Plus, they make portioning out meals for the week a breeze.
- **Taste as You Go:** Your palate is the best tool you have. Regularly taste your food as you cook to adjust the seasoning and flavors. Remember, you can always add more, but you can't take away.

- **Don't Fear the Freezer:** Many recipes in "Campus Cravings" are freezer-friendly. Cook in bulk and freeze portions for later. A freezer meal can be a savior during exam time or when you just don't feel like cooking.
- **Use Technology:** Take advantage of technology. Set timers, use apps for measurement conversions, and don't hesitate to look up a quick tutorial if you're unsure about a technique.
- **The Cleanup:** Clean as you go to avoid a mountain of dishes at the end. Keeping your workspace tidy will make cooking more enjoyable and less of a chore.

Smart Shopping: Tips and Tricks for Budget-Friendly Ingredients
As a student, making the most of your food budget is an essential skill. Here's how you can stretch your dollars further without compromising on the quality or taste of your "Campus Cravings" creations.

- **Plan Ahead:** Create a meal plan before you shop. This keeps you from buying items you don't need and helps prevent waste. Stick to your list, but be flexible enough to take advantage of in-store specials.
- **Buy in Bulk:** Items like rice, pasta, and dried beans are often cheaper in larger quantities. Store them properly, and you'll have a stockpile of staples ready for any recipe.
- **Seasonal Shopping:** Fruits and vegetables are most affordable and flavorful in their peak seasons. Plus, it's a great way to add variety to your meals throughout the year.
- **Go Generic:** Store brands often offer the same quality as name brands for a fraction of the price. Don't pay extra for a label—taste is what matters!
- **Utilize Student Discounts:** Many stores offer discounts to students. Find out which days these apply and plan your shopping accordingly.
- **Local Markets and Farmers:** Visit local farmers' markets close to closing time. You might snag a deal as vendors are more likely to discount produce rather than transport it back.
- **Coupon Savvy:** Keep an eye out for coupons and deals in store flyers or online. Digital coupon apps can also be a great resource for savings.
- **Love the Leftovers:** Get creative with leftovers. A roast chicken can become tomorrow's chicken salad or a hearty soup. This approach maximizes every food purchase.
- **Community Gardens:** If you have access to a community garden, take advantage. Growing your own herbs and veggies is cost-effective and rewarding.
- **Kitchen Share:** Partner with friends to share the cost and quantity of bulk items. This way, you can enjoy a variety without overspending or wasting food.

Implementing these strategies can significantly reduce your grocery bills, making "Campus Cravings" recipes even more economical and enjoyable to prepare. Cooking on a budget doesn't mean you have to sacrifice flavor or nutrition; it just means shopping smarter and getting creative with the resources you have.

Meal Prep 101: A Student's Guide to Time-Saving and Wallet-Friendly Eating

Meal prepping is an essential strategy for students; it saves time, money, and the stress of daily cooking. Here's how you can become a meal prep pro.
Understanding Meal Prep
Meal prep is the concept of preparing whole meals or dishes ahead of schedule. It's particularly popular among busy people because it can help save a lot of time. Having pre-prepared meals on hand can also reduce portion size and help you reach your nutrition goals.

Getting Started

- Choose Your Meals: Pick recipes that are nutritious, filling, and that you enjoy eating. Variety is key to keeping it interesting, so consider prepping different dishes for different days of the week.
- Schedule Your Prep: Set aside a block of time for meal prep. This could be a few hours on a Sunday or any day that fits your schedule.
- Shopping Smart: Make a list based on your meal plan. Buy in bulk where possible, and look for sales and discounts.
- Prep Stations: Organize your ingredients by recipe. Wash, chop, and portion out everything you need before you start cooking.

Cooking and Storing

- Efficient Cooking: Use your oven, stovetop, and any other appliances concurrently to maximize time. For example, roast vegetables in the oven while you cook grains on the stove.
- Portion Control: Divide meals into individual containers. This helps manage portion sizes and makes it easy to grab a meal on the go.
- Proper Storage: Use airtight containers and keep your fridge at the correct temperature to ensure your meals stay fresh throughout the week.

Meal Prep Tips

- Start Simple: If you're new to meal prepping, start with easy recipes that have a short list of ingredients and simple steps.

- Batch Cook: Make large batches of versatile ingredients like rice, pasta, or protein to use in various meals throughout the week.
- Invest in Quality Containers: Durable, microwave-safe containers of various sizes are meal prep essentials.
- Spice It Up: Prevent meal fatigue with different spices, dressings, and toppings to add variety to your meals.
- Freeze for Later: If you like to cook in bulk, freeze portions that you won't eat within the week to keep them fresh.

The Benefits

Meal prepping can transform your eating habits and help you maintain a healthy diet on a student budget. It's a time-saver, money-saver, and an excellent way to learn the ropes of cooking and nutrition. Plus, it's deeply satisfying to know you have a home-cooked meal waiting for you at the end of a long day of lectures. So, gather your containers, plan your menu, and get prepping!

CLASSIC LASAGNA – LAYERS OF LOVE

Verona's Velvet Layers: Dive into layers of pasta, rich meat sauce, creamy béchamel, and melted cheese. A love story on a plate.

🍜 Serves : 2	🍴 Prep Time : 30 Mins	🕐 Cook Time : 45 Mins

Ingredients:

- 12 lasagna sheets
- 500g minced beef
- 1 onion, finely chopped
- 2 garlic cloves, minced
- 400g canned tomatoes
- 2 tbsp tomato paste
- 1 tsp dried oregano
- 1 tsp dried basil
- 500ml béchamel sauce
- 200g mozzarella cheese, shredded
- 50g parmesan cheese, grated
- Salt and black pepper to taste
- Olive oil

Instructions:

- Meat Magic: In a skillet, heat olive oil and sauté the onions and garlic until translucent. Add the minced beef, cooking until browned. Pour in the tomatoes and tomato paste, seasoning with oregano, basil, salt, and pepper. Let it simmer for 20 minutes.
- Layer Love: In a baking dish, spread a scoop of the meat sauce. Place a layer of lasagna sheets over it. Then add more meat sauce, followed by béchamel, and sprinkle with mozzarella and parmesan. Repeat the layers until you run out of ingredients, finishing with cheese on top.
- Baking Beauty: Bake in a preheated oven at 180°C (355°F) for 35-40 minutes or until the top is golden and bubbly.
- Cool & Cut: Let it sit for 10 minutes before serving. This ensures clean cuts.

Alternatives to Jazz it Up:

- Veggie Version: Swap the beef for a mix of zucchini, bell peppers, and mushrooms.
- Spice Surge: Add red pepper flakes for a kick.

COFFEE WALNUT CAKE – A SLICE OF HEAVEN

Bean there, done that: Nothing beats the combo of coffee and walnut in a moist cake slice. Dive in for a caffeine-kick and nutty nirvana all in one!

🥣 Serves : 2	🍴 Prep Time : 20 Mins	🕐 Cook Time : 35 Mins

Ingredients:

- 200g self-raising flour
- 200g unsalted butter, softened
- 200g caster sugar
- 4 eggs
- 2 tbsp instant coffee (dissolved in 1 tbsp hot water)
- 100g walnuts, chopped
- For the icing:
- 200g icing sugar
- 50g unsalted butter, softened
- 1 tbsp instant coffee (dissolved in 1 tsp hot water)
- Chopped walnuts for garnish

Instructions:

- Warm-up & Whisk: Preheat your oven to 180°C (350°F). In a mixing bowl, cream the butter and sugar together until light and fluffy.
- Crack & Combine: Beat in the eggs, one at a time. Add the dissolved coffee and mix thoroughly.
- Fold & Fill: Slowly fold in the self-raising flour and chopped walnuts. Transfer the mixture into a greased cake tin.
- Bake & Bask: Pop it into the oven for 25-30 minutes or until a toothpick comes out clean. Let it cool.
- Icing on Top: For the icing, whip together icing sugar, butter, and dissolved coffee until smooth. Spread over the cooled cake and sprinkle with extra chopped walnuts.
- Slice & Savor: Cut a generous piece, sit back, and enjoy with a steaming mug of coffee or tea!

Alternatives to Jazz it Up:

- Choco-Coffee: Mix in some cocoa powder for a mocha twist.
- Frosty Feels: Add a layer of cream cheese frosting for added richness.

HAM AND CHEESE CROISSANT – MORNING CLASSIC

Crunch & Munch: Why go to France or Pret when this buttery delight can emerge fresh from your oven?

Serves : 2   **Prep Time : 10 Mins**   **Cook Time : 15 Mins**

Ingredients:

- 2 fresh croissants
- 4 slices of quality ham
- 4 slices of Swiss cheese
- 1 tbsp Dijon mustard (optional)

Instructions:

- Preheat & Prep: Warm your oven to 180°C (350°F). Slice the croissants in half, lengthwise.
- Layer & Love: On one half, layer slices of ham and cheese. If desired, spread a thin layer of Dijon mustard on the other half.
- Bake & Bite: Place your prepared croissants on a baking sheet and pop them in the oven for about 5 minutes, or until the cheese is melted and croissant is crispy. Serve immediately!

Alternatives to Jazz it Up:

- Veggie Version: Swap ham for sliced tomatoes and basil for a fresh twist.
- Cheese Choice: Experiment with different cheeses like cheddar or brie.

TUNA SALAD SUB – OCEAN'S BEST

Tuna Triumph: Dive deep into the flavors of the sea with this creamy, crunchy, and utterly delightful sandwich.

🥣 Serves : 2	🍴 Prep Time : 10 Mins	⏱ Cook Time : No Cook

Ingredients:

- 2 sub rolls, split
- 1 can (185g) tuna, drained
- 3 tbsp mayonnaise
- 1 celery stalk, finely chopped
- 1 tbsp red onion, finely chopped
- 1 tsp lemon juice
- Salt and pepper to taste
- Lettuce and sliced tomatoes for garnish

Instructions:

- Mix & Mingle: In a mixing bowl, combine the tuna, mayonnaise, chopped celery, chopped red onion, and lemon juice. Mix well until everything is well incorporated. Season with salt and pepper to taste.
- Load & Layer: Open up your sub rolls and lay a bed of lettuce followed by a couple of tomato slices. Generously pile on your tuna mixture.
- Wrap & Relish: Close up your sub rolls, give them a gentle press to ensure everything stays in, and enjoy every bite of your ocean-inspired delight!

Alternatives to Jazz it Up:

- Herb Harmony: Add some chopped fresh parsley or dill to the tuna mix for a herby touch.
- Crunch Component: Introduce some chopped pickles or capers into your tuna mixture for an added crunch and tang.

CHEEKY CHICKEN WINGS – THE FINGER-LICKING FAVOURITE

Flap and Fly: No need to wing your night out, when you can wing it in style at home! Get your fingers ready for a sticky and spicy delight.

Serves : 4   Prep Time : 10 Mins   Cook Time : 30 Mins

Ingredients:

- 12 chicken wings
- 3 tablespoons peri-peri sauce
- 1 tablespoon honey
- 1 tablespoon olive oil
- Salt to taste

Instructions:

- Saucy Situation: In a big bowl, swirl together the peri-peri sauce, honey, olive oil, and a pinch of salt. Toss the chicken wings in this cheeky mixture until they're well coated.
- Preheat the Oven: Get your oven humming at 200°C.
- Bake Those Babies: Line a baking tray with parchment paper. Lay the wings out, making sure they're not too crowded. Slide them into the oven and bake for 25-30 minutes or until they're golden and crisp.
- Serving Hot: Plate those wings with some extra sauce or a cool yogurt dip. Dive in while they're hot!

Alternatives to Jazz it Up:

- Smoke Signals: Sprinkle a touch of smoked paprika for a smoky depth.
- Tangy Turn: Drizzle a little lime zest or juice for an added zing.
- Grill Game: Fancy some charred edges? Pop these on the grill for the final 5 minutes.

VEGETABLE BIRYANI – THE ROYAL RICE RENDEZVOUS

Basmati's Best: A colorful palette of veggies mingling with fragrant basmati rice and aromatic spices, offering you a plate of royalty.

Serves : 2	Prep Time : 20 Mins	Cook Time : 10 Mins

Ingredients:

- 2 cups basmati rice
- 1 onion, thinly sliced
- 1 cup mixed veggies (carrots, beans, peas, bell peppers, etc.)
- 2 tbsp biryani masala (store-bought)
- 4 cups water
- 2 tbsp oil or ghee
- Fresh mint and coriander leaves, chopped
- 1 bay leaf
- 3-4 cloves
- 2 green cardamom
- 1 black cardamom
- Salt to taste

Instructions:

- Rice's Royal Bath: Wash the basmati rice thoroughly in cold water until the water runs clear. Soak it for about 30 minutes.
- Onion Orchestra: In a deep pan, heat the oil or ghee and fry the sliced onions until golden brown. Keep some aside for garnish.
- Veggie Voyage: Add in the mixed veggies, and sauté for a few minutes.
- Spice Soiree: Sprinkle in the biryani masala, bay leaf, cloves, and cardamoms. Mix well to ensure the veggies are well coated.
- Rice Reveal: Drain the soaked rice and introduce it to the pan. Stir gently.
- Steamy Session: Pour in the water, salt, and bring it to a boil. Once most of the water evaporates, reduce the heat to low, cover the pan, and let the rice cook for another 10-12 minutes.
- Garnish & Grub: Garnish with the fried onions, fresh mint, and coriander leaves. Serve hot with raita or a side salad.

Alternatives to Jazz it Up:

- Nutty Notes: Garnish with some fried cashews and raisins for a royal touch.
- Saffron Streak: Soak a few strands of saffron in warm milk and drizzle over the biryani for added aroma and color.

LEMON HERB GRILLED TOFU – VEGGIE'S PERI DELIGHT

Tofu Transformation: Think tofu is bland? Think again! We're turning this humble veggie staple into a peri-peri star. Say tofu-lly delicious!

Serves : 4   Prep Time : 10 Mins   Cook Time : 15 Mins

Ingredients:

- 400g firm tofu, pressed and sliced into rectangles
- 3 tablespoons peri-peri sauce
- 2 tablespoons lemon juice
- 1 tablespoon fresh herbs (like rosemary, thyme, or parsley), finely chopped
- 1 tablespoon olive oil
- Salt to taste

Instructions:

- Tofu Time: Once you've pressed the tofu (to remove excess water), slice it into even rectangles. This shape will make it easy-peasy to grill.
- Herb Haven: Mix the peri-peri sauce, lemon juice, finely chopped herbs, olive oil, and a pinch of salt in a bowl. Bathe the tofu slices in this mix and let them marinate for at least 30 minutes.
- Grill & Thrill: Preheat your grill or pan to a medium heat. Lay the tofu slices down and let them sizzle for about 4-5 minutes each side, or until they have those dashing grill marks.
- Serve in Style: Plate up your grilled tofu, maybe with a side salad or some saucy dip. Take a bite and let those flavors dance!

Alternatives to Jazz it Up:

- Spice Sprinkle: Top the tofu with some red pepper flakes for an added heat element.
- Asian Twist: Add a splash of soy sauce and a sprinkle of sesame seeds to the marinade for an East meets West delight.
- BBQ Bliss: Baste the tofu with some BBQ sauce in the last few minutes of grilling for a smoky sweetness.

FETTUCCINE ALFREDO – CREAMY PASTA PERFECTION

Roman Resplendence: A dish that sings the creamy tales of Rome. Pasta drenched in a heavenly white sauce.

Serves : 2 | Prep Time : 10 Mins | Cook Time : 20 Mins

Ingredients:

- 250g fettuccine pasta
- 1 cup heavy cream
- 50g unsalted butter
- 1 cup parmesan cheese, grated
- Salt and black pepper to taste
- Fresh parsley, chopped (for garnish)

Instructions:

- Pasta Prep: Boil the fettuccine as per the package instructions until al dente. Drain and keep aside.
- Sauce Splendor: In a saucepan, melt the butter. Pour in the heavy cream and bring to a simmer. Reduce the heat and stir in the grated parmesan until the sauce is smooth and thick.
- Merge Magic: Add the drained pasta to the sauce, tossing to coat every strand. Season with salt and black pepper.
- Plate & Praise: Serve hot, garnished with fresh parsley.

Alternatives to Jazz it Up:

- Garlic Grace: Sauté minced garlic in the butter for added depth.
- Protein Punch: Toss in some grilled chicken strips or sautéed shrimp.

CRISPY SPRING ROLLS - CRUNCHY LITTLE DELIGHTS

Rolling in Flavour: Forget the freezer aisle! These homemade bites will have you rolling in culinary glee

Serves : 4 | Prep Time : 25 Mins | Cook Time : 20 Mins

Ingredients:

- 8 spring roll wrappers
- 50g shredded cabbage
- 50g julienned carrots
- 50g thinly sliced bell peppers
- 1 garlic clove, minced
- 1 tablespoon soy sauce
- Oil for frying

Instructions:

- Veggie Mingle: In a pan over medium heat, sauté your veggies and garlic until they just soften. Drizzle in the soy sauce, give it a twirl, and set aside to cool.
- Roll Call: Once the filling has cooled down, it's time to get rolling. Place a spoonful of filling on each wrapper, tuck and roll tight.
- Fry Fest: Heat your oil in a deep pan or fryer. Once it's shimmering and ready, gently slide in your rolls. Fry until they're golden brown and irresistibly crunchy.

Alternatives to Jazz it Up:

- Dipping Delight: Serve with a tangy tamarind or sweet chilli dip.
- Meaty Mix: Add some minced chicken or prawns to the veggie mix for a heartier bite.

SWEET AND SOUR PRAWN STIR FRY – A TANGY TEASE

Stir-Fry Fly-By: Who needs a takeaway menu when your kitchen can turn into the best Asian eatery in town? This dish is as vibrant in taste as it is in colour.

| 🥣 Serves : 4 | 🍴 Prep Time : 15 Mins | 🕐 Cook Time : 15 Mins |

Ingredients:

- 200g prawns, peeled and deveined
- 1 bell pepper, cubed
- 1 onion, cubed
- 2 tablespoons pineapple chunks
- 3 tablespoons sweet and sour sauce (store-bought for ease)
- 1 tablespoon oil
- Spring onions for garnish, finely chopped

Instructions:

- Prawn Prep: First, let's give those prawns a quick sear in a hot wok with a splash of oil, just until they turn pink. Scoop them out and set aside.
- Veggie Venture: In the same wok, throw in your bell peppers and onions. Stir them around until they soften slightly but still have that crunch.
- Saucy Affair: It's time to bring in the tang! Pour in your sweet and sour sauce, add those pineapple chunks and return the prawns to the wok. Give it a good mix until everything is coated and glistening.
- Plate & Praise: Dish it out and sprinkle some spring onions on top for that finishing touch.

Alternatives to Jazz it Up:

- Go Nuts: Add a sprinkle of crushed peanuts or cashews for an extra crunch.
- Veggie Vault: You can always throw in some snap peas, baby corn, or any other veggies of your choice.

SHEPHERDS PIE – PASTORAL PERFECTION

Field to Fork Delight: No shepherds were harmed in the making of this pie! A comforting concoction of minced meat and mashed potato – truly the stuff of dreams.

🥣 Serves : 2	🍴 Prep Time : 30 Mins	⏲ Cook Time : 40 Mins

Ingredients:

- 500g minced lamb
- 1 onion, chopped
- 2 carrots, diced
- 150g peas
- 1 tbsp tomato paste
- 500ml beef broth
- 2 tsp Worcestershire sauce
- 4 large potatoes, boiled and mashed
- 50g butter
- Salt and pepper to taste
- 2 tbsp oil

Instructions:

- Lamb Layers: In a pan, heat oil and sauté onions until translucent. Add the minced lamb and cook until browned. Drain any excess fat.
- Veggie Volume: Add carrots, peas, tomato paste, and Worcestershire sauce. Pour in the beef broth. Simmer until the liquid has reduced.
- Mash Magic: Mix the boiled and mashed potatoes with butter, salt, and pepper until creamy.
- Pie Process: In a baking dish, layer the lamb mixture at the bottom. Top it off with the mashed potatoes, smoothing the surface.
- Baking Bliss: Bake in a preheated oven at 200°C for 20-25 minutes or until the top is golden. Serve hot and feel the pastoral love!

Alternatives to Jazz it Up:

- Cheese Chase: Sprinkle some grated cheddar on the mashed potatoes before baking for a cheesy twist.
- Herb Hug: Mix in some rosemary or thyme into the lamb mixture for an aromatic touch.

SPICY SZECHUAN NOODLES – FIERY FLAVOR DANCE

Turn up the Heat: No more mundane Monday meals! With these spicy noodles, you'll be adding a sizzle to your week.

🥣 Serves : 4	🍴 Prep Time : 10 Mins	🕐 Cook Time : 15 Mins

Ingredients:

- 200g noodles of your choice
- 2 tablespoons Szechuan sauce (store-bought for ease)
- 1 bell pepper, thinly sliced
- 1 carrot, julienned
- 2 spring onions, sliced
- 1 tablespoon oil
- Sesame seeds for garnish

Instructions:

- Noodle Nook: Cook your noodles as per the packet's instructions, then drain and set them aside.
- Veggie Verve: Heat oil in a wok and toss in bell peppers and carrots. Stir fry until they're slightly tender but still ha2ve a snap.
- Saucy Slide: Pour in the Szechuan sauce, followed by the cooked noodles. Toss everything together until it's all coated in that fiery goodness.
- Serve & Sizzle: Plate your spicy masterpiece and sprinkle some spring onions and sesame seeds on top.

Alternatives to Jazz it Up:

- Protein Punch: Add some grilled chicken strips or pan-fried tofu.
- Green Galore: You can always introduce more veggies – think broccoli florets or snap peas.

BIG MOCK BURGER – YOUR MAIN MEAL MAC

Why Drive-Thru When You Can DIY: Missing that signature burger? Get your buns ready for this juicy mock of a classic!

🥣 Serves : 4	🍴 Prep Time : 20 Mins	🕐 Cook Time : 15 Mins

Ingredients:

- 2 burger buns
- 300g ground beef
- 4 slices of cheddar cheese
- Lettuce, finely shredded
- 1 onion, finely diced
- 2 pickles, sliced
- 4 tablespoons mock special sauce (mix mayo, ketchup, and a hint of mustard)
- Salt and pepper to taste
- 1 tablespoon oil for frying

Instructions:

- Burger Bliss: Season your ground beef with salt and pepper. Mold them into patties.
- Golden Griddle: Heat up a skillet with a touch of oil and place your patties on it. Cook until you achieve that perfect sear on both sides. Top with cheese slices while the second side cooks.
- Assembly Alley: On your bottom bun, spread some special sauce, add lettuce, pickles, and onions. Gently place your cheesy patty on top, followed by the top bun.
- Feast & Fry: Serve with some crispy fries on the side and dive into your homemade drive-thru experience.

Alternatives to Jazz it Up:

- Go Double: Feeling famished? Stack two patties for a double mock experience!
- Veggie Venture: Swap out beef patties for a portobello mushroom or a bean patty for a veggie delight.

CRISPY CHICKEN DELUXE – CLUCKIN' DELICIOUS

Fowl Play in Your Kitchen: Who knew golden, crispy chicken could be recreated so easily at home? Let's cluck to it!

| 🥣 Serves : 4 | ✖️ Prep Time : 15 Mins | 🕐 Cook Time : 20 Mins |

Ingredients:

- 2 chicken breasts
- 1 cup breadcrumbs
- 1 egg, beaten
- Salt and pepper to taste
- Lettuce, for garnish
- Tomato, sliced
- 2 cheese slices
- 2 tablespoons mayo
- 1 tablespoon oil for frying

Instructions:

- Chicken Charm: Season your chicken breasts with salt and pepper, then dip in the beaten egg and roll in the breadcrumbs.
- Golden Goal: In a skillet, heat oil and fry the chicken until it's golden brown and fully cooked.
- Deluxe Dressing: On your bun, spread mayo, place lettuce, then your crispy chicken, followed by tomato slices and cheese.
- Dive In: Pair with some coleslaw on the side and enjoy your deluxe dining.

Alternatives to Jazz it Up:

- Spice Slice: Add some jalapeños for an extra kick.
- Saucy Spin: Swap mayo for BBQ sauce for a tangy twist.

QUINOA SALAD WONDER – A BOWL OF GOODNESS

Quirky Quinoa: Dive into this protein-packed, vibrant bowl. Who knew health could taste so amazing?

🥣 Serves : 2	🍴 Prep Time : 20 Mins	⏱ Cook Time :No Cook

Ingredients:

- 200g quinoa, cooked
- 1 cucumber, diced
- 1 red bell pepper, diced
- 100g cherry tomatoes, halved
- 50g feta cheese, crumbled
- 50g olives, pitted and halved
- 3 tbsp olive oil
- 1 tbsp lemon juice
- Salt and pepper to taste
- Fresh parsley, chopped for garnish

Instructions:

- Toss & Taste: In a large mixing bowl, combine quinoa, cucumber, bell pepper, cherry tomatoes, feta cheese, and olives.
- Dress & Dazzle: In a separate small bowl, whisk together olive oil, lemon juice, salt, and pepper. Pour this dressing over the salad and give it a good mix.
- Serve & Smile: Dish out your quinoa wonder into bowls, garnish with fresh parsley, and take a moment to relish the rainbow!

Alternatives to Jazz it Up:

- Protein Punch: Add grilled chicken or chickpeas for extra satiety.
- Nutty Notion: Toss in some toasted almonds or walnuts for a crunch factor.

APPLE TURNOVER TREAT – SWEET, GOLDEN POCKETS

aA Frui-licious Finale: Why wait for dessert when you can turn over a new leaf and make this at home? Let's get apple-tastic!

🥣 Serves : 4	🍴 Prep Time : 20 Mins	🕐 Cook Time : 25 Mins

Ingredients:

- 2 apples, peeled, cored, and diced
- 2 tablespoons brown sugar
- 1 teaspoon cinnamon
- 1 sheet of puff pastry
- 1 egg (for egg wash)

Instructions:

- Apple Affair: In a pan, mix your diced apples with brown sugar and cinnamon. Cook until they're soft and caramelised.
- Pocket Prep: Roll out your puff pastry and cut into squares. Place a spoonful of apple filling in the center of each square.
- Twist & Turn: Fold over the pastry to form a triangle. Press the edges to seal and brush the top with an egg wash for a golden finish.
- Golden Goodness: Bake in a preheated oven at 200°C for 15-20 minutes or until puffed and golden.
- Tasty Turnover: Allow to cool slightly, sprinkle with some powdered sugar, and enjoy a warm bite!

Alternatives to Jazz it Up:

- Berry Burst: Swap apples for mixed berries for a tangy turnover treat.
- Caramel Core: Drizzle some caramel sauce inside for added sweetness.

FILLET-O-FISH DUPE - DIVE INTO DELIGHT

Fish & Flips: Why fish for compliments when your cooking will reel them in? It's time to cast the culinary net!

Serves : 4	Prep Time : 15 Mins	Cook Time : 10 Mins

Ingredients:

- 2 fish fillets (like cod or haddock)
- 1 cup breadcrumbs
- 1 egg, beaten
- 2 slices of cheddar cheese
- 2 tablespoons tartar sauce
- Lettuce, for garnish
- Salt and pepper to taste
- 1 tablespoon oil for frying

Instructions:

- Fillet Fun: Season your fish fillets with salt and pepper. Dip them in the beaten egg and coat with breadcrumbs.
- Crispy Catch: In a frying pan, heat the oil and cook the fillets until golden and crispy on both sides.
- Layer & Lay: Spread tartar sauce on your bun, place lettuce, and then slide in your crispy fillet. Top it with cheese and the other half of the bun.
- Seafood & Eat It: Serve immediately with a side of tartar dip and enjoy the oceanic orchestra in your mouth!

Alternatives to Jazz it Up:

- Zesty Zing: Add a squeeze of lemon inside for that fresh zing.
- Go Green: Replace lettuce with fresh spinach or rocket for a peppery twist.

CLASSIC CAPPUCCINO – A FOAMY AFFAIR

Stay Grounded: With this brew-tiful beverage, you won't need to step out for your caffeine fix. Let's steam things up!

🥣 Serves : 4	🍴 Prep Time : 5 Mins	🕐 Cook Time : 5 Mins

Ingredients:

- 2 cups of freshly brewed espresso
- 2 cups of milk
- Cocoa powder or cinnamon for garnish

Instructions:

- Espresso Express: Begin by brewing your espresso using your favorite method.
- Milk Magic: In a saucepan or with a steamer, heat your milk until hot but not boiling. Froth it up until it's nice and foamy using a milk frother or by shaking it in a sealed jar.
- Pour & Present: Pour the espresso into your favorite mugs. Slowly add the hot milk, holding back the foam with a spoon. Spoon the foam on top.
- Garnish & Go: Sprinkle with a touch of cocoa powder or cinnamon. Now, sip back and relax!

Alternatives to Jazz it Up:

- Sweeten the Sip: Add a shot of vanilla or caramel syrup for some sweet notes.
- Vegan Victory: Use almond, soy, or oat milk for a dairy-free delight.

BLUEBERRY BLISS MUFFIN – BERRY DELICIOUS!

Muffin to Worry About: Miss the aroma of freshly baked muffins? Here's how to get muffin-tastic right at home!

Serves : 12   Prep Time : 15 Mins   Cook Time : 20 Mins

Ingredients:

- 2 cups all-purpose flour
- 1/2 cup granulated sugar
- 2 tsp baking powder
- 1/2 tsp baking soda
- 1/4 tsp salt
- 1 cup fresh blueberries
- 1 cup buttermilk
- 1/4 cup melted butter
- 1 large egg

Instructions:

- Prep & Preheat: Start by preheating your oven to 190°C (375°F). Line your muffin tin with paper liners or give them a light greasing.
- Mix & Mingle: In a large bowl, whisk together flour, sugar, baking powder, baking soda, and salt. Gently fold in blueberries.
- Wet & Whisk: In another bowl, combine buttermilk, melted butter, and the egg. Pour this wet mixture into your dry ingredients and stir just until combined.
- Bake & Bite: Pour the batter into the muffin tins and bake for 20-25 minutes or until a toothpick inserted comes out clean.
- Muffin Moment: Allow to cool slightly, and enjoy your berry bliss with a steaming cuppa!

Alternatives to Jazz it Up:

- Nutty Note: Add a handful of chopped nuts for some crunch.
- Chocoberry: Mix in some chocolate chips for a sweet surprise.

CLASSIC BLT SUB - BACON LOVER'S THRONE

Bacon Bliss: The iconic trio - Bacon, Lettuce, and Tomato - finds its rightful place in this classic sub. It's simple, it's delicious, and it's a must!

Serves : 2 | Prep Time : 10 Mins | Cook Time : No Cook

Ingredients:

- 2 sub rolls, split
- 8 slices of bacon, cooked until crispy
- 4 lettuce leaves, shredded
- 2 tomatoes, sliced
- 2 tbsp mayonnaise
- Salt and pepper to taste

Instructions:

- Spread & Start: Begin by evenly spreading mayonnaise on the insides of your sub rolls.
- Bacon's Stage: Lay down your crispy bacon slices on the bottom half of the rolls.
- Lettuce & Tomato Tango: On top of the bacon, add your shredded lettuce and tomato slices. Season with salt and pepper.
- Press & Partake: Close up your sub rolls, give them a light press to meld the flavors, and dive into the evergreen taste of a BLT.

Alternatives to Jazz it Up:

- Avocado Adventure: Add slices of ripe avocado for a creamy and healthy touch.
- Sauce Soiree: For an extra layer of flavor, introduce some BBQ sauce, honey mustard, or even a spicy sriracha mayo!

CHILLED FRAPPUCCINO DUPE – COOL BEANS!

Freeze & Please: Forget the fancy equipment. All you need is a blender, some beans, and a little imagination to recreate this chilled charm.

🥣 Serves : 2   ✕ Prep Time : 15 Mins   🕐 Cook Time : No Cook

Ingredients:

- 1 cup strong brewed coffee, cooled
- 1/2 cup milk (of your choice)
- 3 tbsp granulated sugar
- 1 cup ice cubes
- Whipped cream for topping
- Chocolate or caramel syrup for drizzling (optional)

Instructions:

- Blend & Bond: In a blender, combine the cooled coffee, milk, sugar, and ice cubes. Blend until smooth and frothy.
- Pour & Praise: Pour your frosty mixture into glasses. Top with a hefty dollop of whipped cream.
- Drizzle & Dazzle: For that coffee house touch, drizzle with your choice of syrup.
- Sip & Soothe: Grab a straw, take a sip, and let the chill vibes roll!

Alternatives to Jazz it Up:

- Nutty Nudge: Add a spoonful of peanut butter or almond butter for a nutty twist.
- Berry Blast: Blend in some frozen berries for a fruity frapp.

HOT CHOCOLATE EXTRAVAGANZA – CHOCOLATEY EMBRACE

Cocoa Coma: Who needs Starbeans when you can whip up this luxurious, steamy cocoa treat right in your comfy space? Perfect for rainy afternoons or just any time you fancy!

🥣 Serves : 2	🍴 Prep Time : 5 Mins	🕐 Cook Time : 5 Mins

Ingredients:

- 2 cups milk (of your choice)
- 100g dark chocolate, chopped
- 2 tbsp cocoa powder
- 2 tbsp sugar (adjust to taste)
- Pinch of salt
- Whipped cream and chocolate shavings for garnish

Instructions:

- Heat & Hug: In a saucepan, gently heat the milk but don't let it boil.
- Melt & Merge: Add the chopped dark chocolate, cocoa powder, sugar, and a pinch of salt. Whisk continuously until the chocolate is completely melted and the mixture is smooth.
- Pour & Pile: Transfer your rich hot chocolate into mugs.
- Garnish & Gobble: Top it off with a generous amount of whipped cream, sprinkle some chocolate shavings, and there you have it - a hug in a mug!

Alternatives to Jazz it Up:

- Spicy Sip: Add a dash of cinnamon or a pinch of chili powder for an unexpected kick.
- Minty Moment: A drop of peppermint extract can change the game - refreshing and warm at the same time!

CHICKEN POPCORN – BITE-SIZED BLISS

Pop & Lock: Perfect for snacking, these little bites will have you coming back for more and more!

Serves : 2	Prep Time : 15 Mins	Cook Time : 20 Mins

Ingredients:

- 300g chicken breast, cut into bite-sized pieces
- 150g all-purpose flour
- 1 tsp onion powder
- 1 tsp garlic powder
- 1/2 tsp salt
- 1/2 tsp black pepper
- 200ml buttermilk
- Vegetable oil for frying

Instructions:

- Soak & Set: Dunk chicken pieces in buttermilk and let them soak for 30 minutes.
- Flour & Flavor: In a separate bowl, mix flour, onion powder, garlic powder, salt, and pepper.
- Dip & Dredge: Take chicken pieces out of buttermilk, let excess drip off, then coat in the flour mixture.
- Sizzle & Serve: Heat oil in a deep skillet and fry the chicken pieces until golden and crispy. Drain on kitchen paper and serve!

Alternatives to Jazz it Up:

- Cheesy Cheer: Add some grated parmesan to the flour mixture for a cheesy twist.
- Herb Hug: Toss fried pieces with some chopped fresh herbs like parsley or dill.

PANEER BUTTER MASALA - THE VEGETARIAN'S VICTORY

Paneer Pleasure: Let the soft cubes of paneer (cottage cheese) float in a creamy tomato gravy, making you forget all about meat.

Serves : 2 | **Prep Time : 30 Mins** | **Cook Time : 45 Mins**

Ingredients:

- 250g paneer cubes
- 2 tomatoes, pureed
- 2 onions, finely chopped
- 3 garlic cloves, minced
- 1 inch ginger, grated
- 50g butter
- 100ml heavy cream
- 2 tsp garam masala
- 2 tbsp kasuri methi (dried fenugreek leaves)
- Fresh coriander for garnish
- Salt to taste

Instructions:

- Butter Bliss: In a pan, melt the butter and sauté onions until translucent. Add in the garlic and ginger, frying until fragrant.
- Tomato Tango: Pour in the tomato puree, mix, and let it simmer until the oil starts to separate.
- Paneer Party: Introduce the paneer cubes and garam masala. Mix gently to avoid breaking the paneer.
- Creamy Cascade: Add the heavy cream and kasuri methi, stirring gently. Let it simmer for 5-7 minutes.
- Garnish & Gobble: Season with salt, garnish with coriander, and indulge!

Alternatives to Jazz it Up:

- Greens Galore: Toss in some peas or spinach for added color and nutrition.
- Heat Hunt: Add some red chili powder or chopped green chilies for a spicy kick.

SPICY TUNA ROLL – FIERY FISH FANTASY

Turn up the Temp: When regular sushi just won't cut it, this roll brings the fire to your table and zest to your taste buds.

🥣 Serves : 2	🍴 Prep Time : 30 Mins	🕐 Cook Time :No Cook

Ingredients:

- 2 nori sheets
- 200g sushi rice, cooked and seasoned
- 100g fresh tuna, finely chopped
- 1 tbsp spicy mayo
- 1 spring onion, finely chopped

Instructions:

- Rice & Roll: Just as with the California Roll, spread your rice evenly over the nori. But this time, leave a small strip rice-free at the top to help seal the roll.
- Mix & Mingle: In a bowl, mix your chopped tuna, spicy mayo, and spring onion until well combined.
- Place & Press: Place your spicy tuna mix down the center of your rice. Roll it tight using your sushi mat.
- Slice & Serve: With a damp knife, cut into 8 pieces, and serve with soy sauce and extra spicy mayo.

Alternatives to Jazz it Up:

- Cucumber Cool: For a refreshing crunch, add some thin cucumber strips inside your roll.
- Avocado Add-On: A few slices of avocado inside the roll give a creamy contrast to the spicy tuna.

LAMB ROGAN JOSH – THE ROYAL RENDEZVOUS

Lamb's Lush Affair: Tender pieces of lamb drenched in a rich, aromatic curry - a regal experience!

| Serves : 2 | Prep Time : 30 Mins | Cook Time : 60 Mins |

Ingredients:

- 500g lamb pieces
- 2 onions, finely sliced
- 3 garlic cloves, minced
- 1 inch ginger, grated
- 2 tbsp rogan josh spice mix (store-bought)
- 1 cup yogurt, whisked
- 2 tbsp oil
- Fresh coriander for garnish
- Salt to taste

Instructions:

- Onion Odyssey: In a deep pan, heat the oil and fry the sliced onions until they turn golden brown.
- Lamb Land: Add the lamb pieces and brown them on all sides.
- Spice Soak: Sprinkle the rogan josh spice mix, ensuring each lamb piece gets its fair share of spices. Fry for a couple of minutes.
- Yogurt Yacht: Gently pour in the whisked yogurt, mix well, and let it simmer covered for about 25-30 minutes until the lamb is tender and the gravy thickens.
- Finish & Flourish: Season with salt, garnish with fresh coriander, and serve piping hot.

Alternatives to Jazz it Up:

- Potato Plot: Add in some diced potatoes along with the lamb for added texture.
- Nutty Notion: Introduce a handful of cashew paste for a richer and creamier gravy.

PANEER BUTTER MASALA - THE VEGETARIAN'S VICTORY

Paneer Pleasure: Let the soft cubes of paneer (cottage cheese) float in a creamy tomato gravy, making you forget all about meat.

Serves : 2　　Prep Time : 20 Mins　　Cook Time : 30 Mins

Ingredients:

- 250g paneer cubes
- 2 tomatoes, pureed
- 2 onions, finely chopped
- 3 garlic cloves, minced
- 1 inch ginger, grated
- 50g butter
- 100ml heavy cream
- 2 tsp garam masala
- 2 tbsp kasuri methi (dried fenugreek leaves)
- Fresh coriander for garnish
- Salt to taste

Instructions:

- Butter Bliss: In a pan, melt the butter and sauté onions until translucent. Add in the garlic and ginger, frying until fragrant.
- Tomato Tango: Pour in the tomato puree, mix, and let it simmer until the oil starts to separate.
- Paneer Party: Introduce the paneer cubes and garam masala. Mix gently to avoid breaking the paneer.
- Creamy Cascade: Add the heavy cream and kasuri methi, stirring gently. Let it simmer for 5-7 minutes.
- Garnish & Gobble: Season with salt, garnish with coriander, and indulge!

Alternatives to Jazz it Up:

- Greens Galore: Toss in some peas or spinach for added color and nutrition.
- Heat Hunt: Add some red chili powder or chopped green chilies for a spicy kick.

QUICHE LORRAINE – A SAVORY SLICE OF FRANCE

Creamy & Dreamy: This rich pie, with bacon, cheese, and a delightful custard filling, is the belle of the brunch table.

Serves : 2   Prep Time : 25 Mins   Cook Time : 45 Mins

Ingredients:

- 1 pie crust
- 150g bacon, chopped
- 100g Gruyère cheese, grated
- 3 eggs
- 200ml heavy cream
- Salt, pepper, and nutmeg

Instructions:

- Bacon Boost: In a skillet, cook the bacon until crispy. Drain and set aside.
- Custard Creation: In a bowl, whisk together eggs, cream, and seasonings.
- Assemble & Bake: Lay the bacon and cheese on the pie crust. Pour over the egg mixture. Bake in a preheated oven at 180°C for 35-40 minutes, or until set.
- Cool & Cut: Allow the quiche to cool slightly before slicing and serving.

Alternatives to Jazz it Up:

- Veggie Verve: Replace bacon with sautéed mushrooms and spinach.
- Herby Heart: Add some fresh herbs like chives or parsley for a refreshing twist.

CRÈME BRÛLÉE – SWEET, SILKY INDULGENCE

Romance in a Ramekin: This creamy custard topped with a layer of crisp caramel is the very definition of dessert decadence.

Serves : 2 ⁣ Prep Time : 20 Mins ⁣ Cook Time : 40 Mins

Ingredients:

- 500ml heavy cream
- 1 vanilla pod, split and seeds scraped out
- 100g granulated sugar
- 6 egg yolks
- 4 tbsp caster sugar (for the caramel top)

Instructions:

- Creamy Beginning: In a saucepan, heat the cream and vanilla pod (and its seeds) until it's about to boil. Remove from heat and let it infuse for a few minutes.
- Yolk Yum: Whisk egg yolks and granulated sugar until well combined. Slowly add the cream to the mix, stirring constantly.
- Pour & Prepare: Strain the mixture to remove the vanilla pod and divide it among 4 ramekins. Place ramekins in a baking dish and pour boiling water halfway up their sides.
- Bake & Brûlée: Bake in a preheated oven at 150°C for about 40 minutes or until set but still slightly wobbly in the center. Once cooled, refrigerate for a few hours. Sprinkle each with caster sugar and caramelize with a torch until golden and crisp.

Alternatives to Jazz it Up:

- Coffee Kick: Infuse the cream with a couple of tablespoons of strong brewed coffee for a café twist.
- Berry Beautiful: Add some fresh raspberries or blueberries at the base of each ramekin for a fruity surprise.

FRENCH ONION SOUP – A BOWL OF PARISIAN WARMTH

Dive into Depth: Caramelized onions simmered in rich broth, topped with cheesy croutons; this soup is a hug in a bowl.

| 🥣 Serves : 2 | 🍴 Prep Time : 20 Mins | 🕐 Cook Time : 60 Mins |

Ingredients:

- 4 large onions, thinly sliced
- 2 tbsp butter
- 1 tsp sugar
- 1.5 liters beef or vegetable broth
- 200ml white wine
- 4 slices of baguette
- 100g Gruyère cheese, grated
- Salt and pepper

Instructions:

- Onion Odyssey: In a large pot, melt butter and add the onions. Cook slowly until they are deeply caramelized. Add sugar in the latter stages to help the process.
- Broth & Booze: Pour in the wine, and let it reduce by half. Add the broth, season with salt and pepper, and let it simmer for about 30 minutes.
- Cheesy Croutons: Toast the baguette slices until golden, sprinkle generously with Gruyère cheese, and broil until melted and bubbly.
- Serve with Style: Ladle the soup into bowls and float a cheesy crouton on top.

Alternatives to Jazz it Up:

- Herb Haven: Add some fresh thyme and bay leaves while simmering for added aroma.
- Mushroom Magic: Sauté some sliced mushrooms with the onions for an earthy twist.

CHICKEN SHAWARMA – A STREET FOOD STAR

Bite into the Bazaar: Infused with a melange of spices and grilled to perfection, this wrap embodies the vibrant spirit of Middle Eastern streets.

🥣 Serves : 2	🍴 Prep Time : 20 Mins	🕐 Cook Time : 30 Mins

Ingredients:

- 500g boneless chicken thighs, thinly sliced
- 4 tbsp yogurt
- 2 tsp ground cumin
- 2 tsp paprika
- 1 tsp allspice
- 1 tsp ground turmeric
- 1 tsp garlic powder
- 4 flatbreads or pita bread
- Fresh veggies (like lettuce, tomatoes, and onions)
- Tahini or garlic sauce, for drizzling

Instructions:

- Marinate & Wait: Combine chicken with yogurt and all spices. Ensure every piece is well coated. Leave in the refrigerator for a few hours or overnight.
- Grill & Thrill: Skewer the chicken and grill until cooked through and slightly charred. Remove from skewers and slice.
- Wrap & Roll: Lay flatbreads and place veggies, followed by chicken slices. Drizzle your favorite sauce and roll tight.

Alternatives to Jazz it Up:

- Spice Surge: Add some chili powder for an extra kick.
- Cheese Charm: A sprinkle of feta cheese can add a creamy dimension to your wrap.

FALAFEL WRAP – CRISP, CRUNCHY DELIGHT

The Desert's Veggie Gem: These golden crispy balls are the Middle East's answer to vegetarian wonders.

Serves : 2   Prep Time : 20 Mins   Cook Time : 20 Mins

Ingredients:

- 400g canned chickpeas, drained and rinsed
- 1 small onion, chopped
- 2 garlic cloves
- 2 tsp ground cumin
- 1 tsp ground coriander
- 1 tsp chili powder
- 2 tbsp fresh parsley, chopped
- 2 tbsp all-purpose flour
- 4 flatbreads
- Fresh veggies and tahini sauce for serving

Instructions:

- Blend & Bind: In a food processor, combine chickpeas, onion, garlic, spices, parsley, and flour. Pulse until you get a dough-like consistency.
- Shape & Fry: Form small balls or patties from the mixture. Deep fry until golden brown and crisp.
- Assemble & Savor: Place falafels in a flatbread, add veggies, and generously drizzle with tahini sauce. Roll and enjoy.

Alternatives to Jazz it Up:

- Herb Hike: Incorporate fresh cilantro or mint for a fresh twist.
- Oven Option: For a healthier variant, bake the falafels at 200°C until golden.

TOM YUM SOUP – THE TANGY TEMPTRESS

Soupy Splendor: Embark on a tangy, spicy, and aromatic journey with this classic Thai soup, known for its rich flavors and invigorating aroma.

Serves : 2   **Prep Time : 20 Mins**   **Cook Time : 25 Mins**

Ingredients:

- 1 liter chicken or vegetable broth
- 300g shrimp, cleaned and deveined
- 2 stalks lemongrass, smashed and cut into 2-inch lengths
- 5 kaffir lime leaves, torn
- 3 slices galangal
- 4 Thai bird chilies, smashed
- 200g straw mushrooms, halved
- 2 medium tomatoes, quartered
- 1 small red onion, sliced
- 3 tbsp fish sauce
- 1 tbsp lime juice
- 1 tsp sugar
- Fresh cilantro for garnish

Instructions:

- Broth Beginnings: Bring broth to boil, then add lemongrass, galangal, kaffir lime leaves, and chilies. Simmer for 10 minutes to infuse.
- Shrimp & Veggies: Add shrimp, mushrooms, tomatoes, and onion. Cook until the shrimp turns pink.
- Final Flavorings: Stir in fish sauce, lime juice, and sugar. Adjust seasoning as needed. Serve hot, garnished with cilantro.

Alternatives to Jazz it Up:

- Chicken Change: Replace shrimp with chicken strips for a different protein punch.
- Noodle Note: Add rice noodles to transform this into a filling noodle soup.

HUMMUS AND PITA BREAD – THE SULTAN'S SMOOTH DIP

Spread the Love: This creamy chickpea delight is a staple that has conquered global tables.

Serves : 2	Prep Time : 20 Mins	Cook Time : No Cook

Ingredients:

- 400g canned chickpeas, reserve the liquid
- 2 garlic cloves
- 2 tbsp tahini
- 1 lemon's juice
- 2 tbsp olive oil
- Salt to taste
- Pita bread for serving

Instructions:

- Blend & Perfect: In a food processor, blend chickpeas, garlic, tahini, lemon juice, and olive oil. Add the reserved chickpea liquid until desired consistency. Season with salt.
- Serve & Dip: Pour hummus into a bowl, drizzle with a bit more olive oil, and serve with warm pita bread.

Alternatives to Jazz it Up:

- Paprika Pop: A sprinkle of paprika can add a smoky note.
- Pesto Fusion: Mix in some basil pesto for a Mediterranean-Middle Eastern fusion.

BBQ PULLED PORK SANDWICH – THE SAUCY SHOWSTOPPER

A Southern Symphony: Tender pork bathed in a rich BBQ sauce, enveloped by a soft bun, making every bite a testament to patience and passion.

Serves : 2   Prep Time : 20 Mins   Cook Time : 180 Mins

Ingredients:

- 500g pork shoulder
- 200ml BBQ sauce of choice
- 4 soft sandwich buns
- 1 onion, thinly sliced
- Pickles for serving

Instructions:

- Low & Slow: Cook the pork shoulder in a slow cooker for about 8 hours or until it's tender and falls apart easily.
- Pulled Perfection: Once cooked, shred the pork using two forks and mix it with BBQ sauce.
- Assemble & Adore: Place a generous amount of pulled pork on the bottom half of a bun. Top with sliced onions and pickles, then crown with the other half of the bun.

Alternatives to Jazz it Up:

- Spice Seeker: Add some jalapenos for an extra kick.
- Cheese Champion: Melt some cheddar cheese over the pork for a creamy delight.

HICKORY-SMOKED RIBS – RIBBED FOR YOUR PLEASURE

Fall-off-the-Bone Fantastic: These ribs, kissed by the smoke and cradled by the flame, are what barbecue dreams are made of.

Serves : 2   Prep Time : 20 Mins   Cook Time : 120 Mins

Ingredients:

- 4 racks of baby back ribs
- 100g BBQ dry rub
- 200ml BBQ sauce
- Hickory wood chips

Instructions:

- Prep & Rub: Clean the ribs and pat them dry. Apply a generous amount of the BBQ dry rub on both sides.
- Smokin' Hot: In a smoker, add the hickory wood chips and let the ribs smoke for about 5 hours at 225°F (107°C).
- Sauced & Seared: Glaze the ribs with BBQ sauce and sear them on a hot grill for that caramelized finish.

Alternatives to Jazz it Up:

- Sweet & Heat: Opt for a spicy honey BBQ sauce for a tantalizing twist.
- Citrus Sing: Marinate the ribs with a bit of orange or lime zest for a citrusy undertone.

ZÜRCHER GESCHNETZELTES – CREAMY CULINARY CREATION

Tender & Tasty: This Zurich-style sliced meat dish, usually veal, in a creamy mushroom sauce is hearty and delectable.

Serves : 2   **Prep Time : 20 Mins**   **Cook Time : 20 Mins**

Ingredients:

- 500g veal or chicken, thinly sliced
- 1 onion, finely chopped
- 200g mushrooms, sliced
- 200ml heavy cream
- 100ml white wine
- 2 tbsp butter
- 2 tsp lemon juice
- Salt, pepper, and chopped parsley to taste

Instructions:

- Sauté & Set: In a pan, melt butter and sauté the meat until browned. Remove and set aside.
- Sauce & Simmer: In the same pan, add onions and mushrooms. Sauté until softened. Add white wine and reduce. Stir in the cream, lemon juice, and seasonings. Bring to a simmer.
- Combine & Cook: Return the meat to the pan and simmer until everything is heated through and flavors meld.
- Garnish & Serve: Sprinkle with chopped parsley and serve hot, traditionally with Rösti.

Alternatives to Jazz it Up:

- Wine Wonder: Use a good quality wine for a richer flavor.
- Herb Infusion: Add some thyme or rosemary for added depth.

SWISS CHOCOLATE CAKE - CHOCO-CHALET CHARM

Decadent & Delicious: Dive into the rich world of Swiss chocolate with this indulgent cake.

🥣 Serves : 2	🍴 Prep Time : 30 Mins	⏱ Cook Time : 35 Mins

Ingredients:

- 200g Swiss dark chocolate
- 150g unsalted butter
- 200g sugar
- 5 eggs, separated
- 1 tsp vanilla extract
- Pinch of salt

Instructions:

- Melt & Mix: Preheat the oven to 180°C. Melt the chocolate and butter together. Once melted, stir in the sugar, egg yolks, and vanilla.
- Whisk & Fold: In a separate bowl, whisk the egg whites with a pinch of salt until stiff peaks form. Gently fold into the chocolate mixture.
- Bake & Cool: Pour into a greased cake tin and bake for 30-35 minutes. Let it cool before serving.

Alternatives to Jazz it Up:

- Berry Blast: Serve with a side of fresh berries or berry compote.
- Creamy Companion: A dollop of whipped cream or vanilla ice cream pairs wonderfully.

STUFFED GRAPE LEAVES – NILE'S NEAT PARCELS

Delicate Delight: Grape leaves filled with a tangy rice mixture, these are perfect finger foods for any gathering.

Serves : 2   Prep Time : 30 Mins   Cook Time : 40 Mins

Ingredients:

- 20 grape leaves, jarred or fresh
- 1 cup rice, soaked in water for 30 mins
- 1 large tomato, finely chopped
- 1 large onion, finely chopped
- 1/4 cup parsley, finely chopped
- Juice of 1 lemon
- 2 tbsp olive oil
- Salt and pepper to taste

Instructions:

- Filling Prep: In a bowl, mix rice, tomatoes, onions, parsley, lemon juice, olive oil, salt, and pepper.
- Roll & Stuff: Lay out a grape leaf, vein side up. Place a teaspoon of filling in the center. Fold in the sides and roll tightly.
- Cook: Place the stuffed leaves in a pot, seam side down. Cover with water, place a plate on top to keep them submerged. Simmer for 45 mins to 1 hour, until fully cooked.
- Serve: Serve warm or at room temperature with a side of yogurt or tahini sauce.

Alternatives to Jazz it Up:

- Meat Mix: Add some finely minced lamb or beef to the rice mixture for a meaty variation.
- Zesty Zing: Drizzle with some additional lemon juice or zest before serving for added tang.

FALAFEL PATTIES – PHARAOH'S FAVOURITE FRITTERS

Crispy & Crunchy: These deep-fried patties made from ground chickpeas or fava beans are a popular Middle Eastern treat, but Egypt claims them as its own!

🥣 Serves : 2	🍴 Prep Time : 20 Mins	🕐 Cook Time : 20 Mins

Ingredients:

- 200g dried chickpeas, soaked overnight
- 1 small onion, roughly chopped
- 2 cloves garlic
- 2 tbsp fresh coriander, chopped
- 2 tbsp fresh parsley, chopped
- 1 tsp ground cumin
- 1 tsp ground coriander
- 1/2 tsp chili powder
- Salt to taste
- Baking soda, a pinch
- Oil for frying

Instructions:

- Blend & Mix: In a food processor, blend chickpeas, onions, garlic, fresh coriander, parsley, ground spices, salt, and baking soda until a coarse mixture forms.
- Shape & Chill: Shape into small balls or patties. Chill in the refrigerator for at least an hour.
- Fry & Feast: Heat oil in a deep pan. Fry the patties in batches until they are golden brown. Serve hot with tahini sauce or inside pita bread pockets.

Alternatives to Jazz it Up:

- Sesame Sprinkle: Before frying, roll the falafel balls in sesame seeds for an added crunch.
- Herb Boost: Add some fresh dill or mint to the mixture for a refreshing twist.

BASBOUSA (SEMOLINA CAKE) – EGYPTIAN EUPHORIA IN EVERY BITE

Sweet Satisfaction: This classic semolina cake soaked in simple syrup is a delightful dessert that's adored across Egypt.

Serves : 2   **Prep Time : 20 Mins**   **Cook Time : 30 Mins**

Ingredients:

- 250g semolina
- 250g sugar
- 250g yogurt
- 50g unsalted butter, melted
- 1 tsp baking powder
- 50g desiccated coconut (optional)
- Whole almonds for garnish
- Syrup:
- 200g sugar
- 100ml water
- 1 slice of lemon

Instructions:

- Mix & Pour: In a bowl, mix semolina, sugar, yogurt, melted butter, baking powder, and desiccated coconut (if using) until combined. Pour into a greased baking tray.
- Garnish & Bake: Place an almond on each piece. Bake in a preheated oven at 180°C for 30-35 minutes or until golden.
- Syrup Soak: For the syrup, boil sugar, water, and lemon slice until sugar dissolves. Pour the hot syrup over the warm cake. Let it soak in.
- Slice & Serve: Once cooled, slice and serve.

Alternatives to Jazz it Up:

- Rose Romance: Add some rose water to the syrup for a fragrant touch.
- Nutty Nuance: Mix in some crushed pistachios or walnuts into the batter for added crunch.

MOLOKHIA (GREEN SOUP) – NEFERTITI'S NOURISHING NECTAR

Rich & Velvety: Made from the leaves of the jute plant, this green soup is both nutritious and delectable.

🍚 Serves : 2	🍴 Prep Time : 20 Mins	🕐 Cook Time : 40 Mins

Ingredients:

- 400g frozen or fresh molokhia leaves, finely chopped
- 3 cloves garlic, minced
- 1 chicken or rabbit, cut into pieces
- 2 liters chicken stock
- 2 tbsp butter
- Salt, pepper, and ground coriander to taste

Instructions:

- Broth Base: In a large pot, boil the chicken or rabbit in chicken stock until fully cooked. Remove the meat and set aside. Strain the stock to remove any impurities.
- Molokhia Magic: Return the stock to the pot. Add the chopped molokhia leaves. Simmer for 20-30 minutes.
- Garlic Goodness: In a separate pan, sauté the minced garlic in butter until golden. Add ground coriander, salt, and pepper. Mix well.
- Combine & Cook: Add the garlic mixture to the molokhia pot. Let it simmer for an additional 10 minutes.
- Serve & Savor: Serve hot with the boiled meat on the side and accompany with rice or bread.

Alternatives to Jazz it Up:

- Spicy Spin: Add some chili flakes or cayenne pepper for a spicy kick.
- Aromatic Addition: A dash of cumin or a bay leaf can enhance the flavor profile of this traditional soup.

PAD THAI – THE STIR-FRIED SENSATION

Noodle Nirvana: Dive into Thailand's national dish, an ever-popular stir-fry that melds flavors in perfect harmony.

Serves : 2	Prep Time : 20 Mins	Cook Time : 15 Mins

Ingredients:

- 200g flat rice noodles
- 200g prawns, peeled and deveined
- 2 eggs, lightly beaten
- 3 cloves garlic, minced
- 3 shallots, thinly sliced
- 2 tbsp tamarind paste
- 2 tbsp fish sauce
- 1 tbsp palm sugar
- 100g bean sprouts
- 50g roasted peanuts, crushed
- 2 green onions, sliced
- Red chili flakes, to taste
- Lime wedges for serving

Instructions:

- Noodle Prep: Soak rice noodles in warm water for 30 minutes, then drain.
- Sauce Simmer: Mix tamarind paste, fish sauce, and palm sugar in a bowl. Set aside.
- Sauté & Stir: In a wok or large skillet, sauté garlic and shallots. Add prawns and cook until pink. Push to one side and pour in eggs, scrambling them. Add noodles and sauce, tossing everything together.
- Garnish & Go: Top with bean sprouts, peanuts, green onions, and chili flakes. Serve with a lime wedge on the side.

Alternatives to Jazz it Up:

- Tofu Twist: Swap prawns with firm tofu for a vegetarian delight.
- Nut-Free: Replace peanuts with toasted sesame seeds for a different crunch.

GREEN CURRY CHICKEN – THE VERDANT DELIGHT

Tropical Temptation: Dive into this rich, creamy, and aromatic curry that speaks of Thailand's lush landscapes.

Serves : 2   **Prep Time : 20 Mins**   **Cook Time : 25 Mins**

Ingredients:

- 400ml coconut milk
- 500g chicken breast, cubed
- 2 tbsp green curry paste
- 100g Thai eggplants, quartered
- 1 red bell pepper, sliced
- 1 kaffir lime leaf, torn
- 1 tbsp fish sauce
- 1 tsp palm sugar
- Thai basil leaves for garnish

Instructions:

- Coconut Commence: In a pot, bring half of the coconut milk to a simmer. Add green curry paste and mix until well combined.
- Chicken & Veggies: Add chicken cubes and cook until they turn white. Add the remaining coconut milk, eggplants, and bell pepper. Simmer until cooked.
- Final Flavors: Add fish sauce, palm sugar, and kaffir lime leaf. Simmer for a few more minutes.

Alternatives to Jazz it Up:

- Seafood Switch: Use prawns or fish chunks instead of chicken for a coastal twist.
- Veggie Venture: For a vegetable-loaded version, add zucchini, bamboo shoots, and broccoli.

MANGO STICKY RICE – THE SWEET RETREAT

Tropical Transcendence: This dessert is a harmonious pairing of ripe mango and glutinous rice, a love story celebrated on plates across Thailand.

🥣 Serves : 2	🍴 Prep Time : 15 Mins	⏱️ Cook Time : 20 Mins

Ingredients:

- 200g glutinous rice, soaked overnight
- 400ml coconut milk
- 100g palm sugar
- 1 pinch of salt
- 2 ripe mangoes, peeled and sliced
- Toasted sesame seeds or mung beans for garnish

Instructions:

- Rice & Steam: Drain the soaked rice and steam until tender and translucent.
- Sweet Simmer: In a saucepan, combine coconut milk, palm sugar, and salt. Heat until the sugar dissolves but do not boil. Pour half over the cooked rice, letting it absorb the sweet mixture.
- Plate & Present: Serve rice with mango slices and drizzle with the remaining coconut mixture. Sprinkle with toasted sesame seeds or mung beans.

Alternatives to Jazz it Up:

- Berry Bliss: Drizzle some berry coulis over the top for a fruity kick.
- Caramel Cascade: A drizzle of salted caramel can introduce a delightful twist.

VEGETABLE SPRING ROLLS – CRUNCHY COMPANIONS

Crisp Celebrations: These bite-sized delights are perfect as an appetizer or snack, encapsulating the essence of Thai flavors in a crunchy wrap.

🥣 Serves : 2	✕ Prep Time : 30 Mins	🕐 Cook Time : 20 Mins

Ingredients:

- 12 spring roll wrappers
- 100g glass noodles, soaked and drained
- 50g carrots, julienned
- 50g cabbage, shredded
- 50g bean sprouts
- 2 green onions, sliced
- 2 tbsp soy sauce
- 1 tsp sesame oil
- Oil for frying
- Sweet chili sauce for dipping

Instructions:

- Filling Fix: In a pan, sauté carrots, cabbage, bean sprouts, and green onions until slightly soft. Add glass noodles, soy sauce, and sesame oil. Mix well and let cool.
- Roll & Wrap: Place a tablespoon of the filling onto each spring roll wrapper. Fold the sides and roll tightly.
- Fry & Feast: Heat oil in a deep-frying pan and fry the rolls until golden brown. Serve with sweet chili sauce.

Alternatives to Jazz it Up:

- Protein Punch: Add minced chicken or shrimp to the filling.
- Dip Delights: Serve with a peanut or tamarind sauce for varied dipping options.

MOUSSAKA – THE MEDITERRANEAN MARVEL

Layers of Love: Dive into this rich, layered casserole that combines succulent meat, creamy béchamel, and perfectly roasted aubergines.

Serves : 2   **Prep Time : 30 Mins**   **Cook Time : 45 Mins**

Ingredients:

- 3 large aubergines, sliced
- 500g minced lamb or beef
- 1 onion, finely chopped
- 3 garlic cloves, minced
- 400g canned tomatoes
- 2 tbsp tomato paste
- 1 tsp cinnamon
- 1 tsp oregano
- 100g feta cheese, crumbled
- 50g grated parmesan
- Olive oil
- Salt & pepper to taste
- For the Béchamel:
- 50g butter
- 50g flour
- 500ml milk
- 1 pinch of nutmeg

Instructions:

- Aubergine Awe: Lightly salt the aubergine slices and set them aside for 30 minutes. Rinse, pat dry, and fry in olive oil until golden brown. Set aside.
- Meaty Mix: In a pan, sauté onion and garlic until translucent. Add the minced meat and cook until browned. Stir in tomatoes, tomato paste, cinnamon, and oregano. Simmer for 20 minutes. Season to taste.
- Béchamel Brilliance: Melt butter in a saucepan, stir in flour until a smooth paste forms. Gradually add milk, constantly stirring until it thickens. Season with salt, pepper, and a pinch of nutmeg.
- Layer & Bake: In a baking dish, start with a layer of aubergines, followed by the meat mixture, and then béchamel. Repeat. Top with crumbled feta and grated parmesan. Bake at 180°C for 40 minutes or until golden brown.

Alternatives to Jazz it Up:

- Potato Power: Add a layer of thinly sliced potatoes at the base for added heartiness.
- Veggie Version: Replace meat with lentils and mushrooms for a vegetarian take.

SPANAKOPITA (SPINACH PIE) – HELLENIC HEARTY PARCEL

Crispy & Creamy: This delectable pie combines crispy filo pastry with a creamy spinach and feta filling.

Serves : 2   Prep Time : 30 Mins   Cook Time : 35 Mins

Ingredients:

- 500g fresh spinach, washed and chopped
- 200g feta cheese, crumbled
- 2 eggs, beaten
- 1 onion, finely chopped
- 3 tbsp fresh dill, chopped
- 1 pack of filo pastry
- Olive oil or melted butter for brushing
- Salt & pepper to taste

Instructions:

- Spinach Sauté: In a pan, sauté the onion until translucent. Add spinach and cook until wilted. Let cool, then drain any excess liquid.
- Perfect Pie Filling: Mix the cooled spinach, crumbled feta, dill, and beaten eggs. Season to taste.
- Filo Fun: Brush a baking dish with olive oil or butter. Layer 6 sheets of filo, brushing each with oil or butter. Spread the spinach mixture. Top with another 6 sheets of filo, brushing each layer as before. Trim excess and tuck the edges in.
- Golden Goodness: Bake in a preheated oven at 180°C for 35-40 minutes or until golden brown.

Alternatives to Jazz it Up:

- Herby Hints: Add a mix of fresh herbs like mint or parsley for a refreshing twist.
- Meaty Makeover: Incorporate some sautéed ground lamb into the filling for a meaty spin.

CLASSIC VEGGIE WRAP - VEGGIE VIBES

Wrap & Roll: Dive into this vegetable medley with each bite. Fresh, crisp, and utterly delicious!

🥣 Serves : 2	🍴 Prep Time : 15 Mins	⏱️ Cook Time : No Cook

Ingredients:

- 2 large tortilla wraps
- 100g hummus
- 1 cucumber, thinly sliced
- 1 carrot, julienned
- 1 red bell pepper, thinly sliced
- 50g mixed lettuce leaves
- 50g feta cheese, crumbled (skip for vegan version)

Instructions:

- Spread & Stack: Lay out the tortilla and spread a generous layer of hummus. On top, layer cucumber, carrot, bell pepper, lettuce, and feta cheese.
- Wrap Wonder: Roll the tortilla tightly, making sure the fillings stay inside. Cut in half and serve immediately.

Alternatives to Jazz it Up:

- Protein Punch: Add some grilled tofu or tempeh for an extra protein boost.
- Saucy Spin: Drizzle some tahini or sriracha for added flavor.

VEGAN BREAKFAST BITES - A MORNING MIRACLE

Munch Morning, Vegan Style: Kickstart your day with these delightful breakfast bites. No dairy, no problem!

Serves : 2 | Prep Time : 15 Mins | Cook Time : 20 Mins

Ingredients:

- 200g firm tofu, crumbled
- 1 tbsp olive oil
- 1 small onion, finely chopped
- 1/2 red bell pepper, diced
- 1 tsp turmeric (for color)
- Salt and pepper to taste
- 4 vegan sausage links, cooked and chopped
- 4 tortilla wraps

Instructions:

- Sauté & Spice: In a skillet, heat olive oil and sauté onions until translucent. Add bell pepper and cook until softened.
- Tofu Time: Stir in crumbled tofu, turmeric, salt, and pepper. Cook for about 5-7 minutes, stirring occasionally.
- Roll & Relish: Lay out a tortilla wrap, add some tofu scramble and chopped vegan sausage. Roll up tightly and your breakfast bite is ready to be savored!

Alternatives to Jazz it Up:

- Spice Spin: Toss in some smoked paprika or cayenne pepper for a little kick.
- Greens Galore: Spinach or kale can be added for an extra health punch.

MACKIE'S MCFLURRY SURPRISE – SWIRLS OF SWEETNESS

Swirl & Savor: No need to drive-thru when you can stir up this dreamy dessert in a jiffy! Let's freeze the moment, shall we?

Serves : 4   Prep Time : 15 Mins   Cook Time :No cook

Ingredients:

- 4 cups of vanilla ice cream
- 1 cup of your favorite chocolate/candy, chopped (e.g., M&Ms, Oreo pieces)
- 2 tablespoons of chocolate syrup
- Whipped cream for topping (optional)

Instructions:

- Chill Bill: Ensure your ice cream is cold but slightly soft for easy mixing.
- Mix & Match: In a large bowl, combine the slightly softened vanilla ice cream with your chosen chopped candy or chocolate.
- Syrupy Spin: Drizzle in the chocolate syrup and give it a gentle swirl, ensuring you still see those delightful candy pieces.
- Serve & Swirl: Scoop your mixture into serving bowls. Top with a dollop of whipped cream if desired.
- Treat Time: Dive in with a spoon and get lost in the sweet swirls of this homemade McFlurry!

Alternatives to Jazz it Up:

- Fruity Fun: Add in some chopped berries for a fruity twist.
- Nutty Notes: Sprinkle with chopped nuts for added crunch and flavor.

SILKY RAMEN BOWL – THE SOULFUL SOUP

Noodling at Home: No more noodle queues or cold winter walks to the nearest ramen joint. Dive into a steamy bowl of homemade love!

| 🥣 Serves : 4 | 🍴 Prep Time : 15 Mins | 🕐 Cook Time : 20 Mins |

Ingredients:

- 200g ramen noodles
- 1 litre chicken or vegetable broth
- 2 garlic cloves, minced
- 1 tablespoon ginger, minced
- 2 tablespoons soy sauce
- 2 spring onions, thinly sliced
- 100g spinach or bok choy
- 2 soft-boiled eggs, halved
- 100g sliced grilled chicken or tofu

Instructions:

- Broth Beginnings: In a large pot, sauté the minced garlic and ginger until fragrant. Pour in your chosen broth and bring to a gentle simmer.
- Flavour Dive: Infuse the broth with soy sauce. Give it a taste. Needs a tweak? Maybe a touch more salt or another splash of soy?
- Noodle Nest: In a separate pot, follow the ramen packet's dance steps till they're perfectly al dente. Drain and set them aside.

Alternatives to Jazz it Up:

- Heat Hint: For those who like it hot, drizzle in some chilli oil or sprinkle in red pepper flakes.
- Protein Swap: Fancy some pork or beef? Swap out the chicken or tofu. Remember, your bowl, your rules!

PRET'S TOMATO AND FETA SOUP – SOUP-ER BOWL

Sip the Simplicity: A heart-warming bowl, brimming with the tanginess of tomatoes and the richness of feta. Dive in, one spoonful at a time!

Serves : 2 **Prep Time : 15 Mins** **Cook Time : 30 Mins**

Ingredients:

- 800g canned tomatoes
- 1 onion, chopped
- 2 garlic cloves, minced
- 1 liter vegetable stock
- 100g feta cheese, crumbled
- 2 tbsp olive oil
- Salt and pepper to taste
- Fresh basil for garnish

Instructions:

- Sauté Secrets: In a large pot, heat olive oil and sauté onions until translucent. Add garlic and cook for another 2 minutes.
- Tomato Time: Pour in canned tomatoes and vegetable stock. Bring to a boil and then simmer for 20 minutes.
- Blend & Boost: Using an immersion blender, puree the soup until smooth. Stir in crumbled feta and season with salt and pepper.
- Serve & Savor: Pour into bowls, garnish with fresh basil, and enjoy the warmth!

Alternatives to Jazz it Up:

- Spice Spin: Add a pinch of chili flakes for a touch of heat.
- Creamy Crave: Stir in a dollop of yogurt or cream for a velvety finish.

TRADITIONAL IRISH STEW – EIRE'S EDIBLE EMBRACE

From the Heart of Ireland: When the weather turns nippy, nothing warms the soul like this. Dive into a bowl of history and warmth, where the potatoes and meat dance in harmony.

🥣 Serves : 2	🍴 Prep Time : 20 Mins	🕐 Cook Time : 120 Mins

Ingredients:

- 500g lamb, cubed
- 4 large potatoes, sliced
- 2 onions, sliced
- 3 carrots, sliced
- 500ml beef or vegetable broth
- 2 tsp thyme
- 2 tsp parsley
- Salt and pepper to taste
- 2 tbsp oil

Instructions:

- Brown the Basics: In a large pot, heat the oil and brown the lamb cubes. Remove and set aside.
- Veggie Ventures: In the same pot, sauté the onions until translucent. Add carrots and cook for a few more minutes.
- Stewing Starts: Return the browned lamb to the pot. Add potatoes, broth, thyme, and parsley. Season with salt and pepper.
- Slow & Steady: Bring the stew to a boil, then reduce to a simmer. Cover and let it cook for about 1.5 to 2 hours.
- Serve & Savor: Once the meat is tender and the potatoes cooked through, ladle into bowls. Sprinkle some fresh parsley on top for that extra touch. Enjoy with a slice of fresh bread!

Alternatives to Jazz it Up:

- Beefy Boost: Substitute lamb with beef for a different take.
- Guinness Galore: Add a splash of Guinness for depth and a richer flavor.

BOXTY PANCAKES – THE POTATO POETRY

Morning, Noon, or Night: Whether it's breakfast or supper, these traditional Irish potato pancakes hit the right spot every time. Serve 'em up and watch them disappear!

🥣 Serves : 2	🍴 Prep Time : 15 Mins	🕐 Cook Time : 20 Mins

Ingredients:

- 2 large potatoes, grated
- 2 large potatoes, boiled and mashed
- 100g flour
- 1 tsp baking powder
- 200ml milk
- Salt and pepper to taste
- 2 tbsp oil or butter for frying

Instructions:

- Potato Pairing: In a mixing bowl, combine both the grated and mashed potatoes.
- Batter Basics: Stir in the flour, baking powder, milk, salt, and pepper. Mix until you have a smooth batter.
- Pancake Process: Heat oil or butter in a pan. Pour in ladlefuls of the batter to make pancakes. Fry until they are golden on both sides.
- Serve & Swoon: Serve these boxty pancakes hot with a dollop of sour cream or apple sauce. It's an Irish embrace in every bite!

Alternatives to Jazz it Up:

- Savory Spin: Add some grated cheese or chives into the batter for a different flavor profile.
- Sweet Surprise: For a sweet version, skip the pepper and serve with honey or berry compote.

SPICY PERI-PERI PRAWNS – A SEAFOOD SENSATION

Dive Deep: Why sail the seven seas when the ocean's bounty can sizzle in your skillet? Let's get those prawns popping!

🥣 Serves : 4	🍴 Prep Time : 15 Mins	🕐 Cook Time : 10 Mins

Ingredients:

- 300g fresh prawns, deveined and shelled
- 3 tablespoons peri-peri sauce
- 1 tablespoon garlic, finely minced
- 1 tablespoon olive oil
- Freshly chopped parsley for garnish
- Lemon wedges for serving

Instructions:

- Marinade Magic: Whisk together peri-peri sauce, garlic, and olive oil in a bowl. Toss in the prawns and ensure they're well coated. Let them soak up the flavors for about 30 minutes.
- Sizzle Time: Heat a skillet or pan over medium-high heat. Once hot, throw in the prawns. Cook for 2-3 minutes on each side or until they turn a lovely pink.
- Plate & Serve: Dish out those prawns, sprinkle some fresh parsley, and squeeze a lemon wedge for that zesty finish. Dive in!

Alternatives to Jazz it Up:

- Buttery Bliss: Add a knob of butter while cooking for a richer taste.
- Herb Hug: Mix in some chopped dill or coriander for a fresh twist.
- Skewer Style: Thread these on skewers and grill them for a barbecue touch.

FIERY GRILLED CHICKEN – A FLAME-GRILLED FAVOURITE

Grill Thrills: Why wait in line when you can have this grilled wonder sizzling on your plate? Turn on the grill and let's create some cheeky magic!

🥣 Serves : 4	🍴 Prep Time : 25 Mins	🕐 Cook Time : 20 Mins

Ingredients:

- 4 chicken breasts
- 4 tablespoons peri-peri sauce
- 2 tablespoons olive oil
- 1 tablespoon lemon juice
- Salt and freshly ground black pepper, to taste

Instructions:

- Marinade Magic: In a bowl, combine the peri-peri sauce, olive oil, lemon juice, salt, and pepper. Mix it up and then coat the chicken breasts generously with the marinade. Let these sit for at least an hour (the longer, the spicier!).
- Get Grilling: Preheat your grill to medium-high. Once hot, place the marinated chicken breasts on the grill. Cook each side for about 7-8 minutes or until the chicken is fully cooked and has those beautiful grill marks.
- Rest & Serve: Allow the grilled chicken to rest for a few minutes before slicing. Serve it with some extra peri-peri sauce on the side and perhaps a refreshing salad!

Alternatives to Jazz it Up:

- Spice Levels: Adjust the peri-peri sauce quantity to match your heat preference.
- Herbaceous Touch: Mix in some finely chopped fresh coriander or parsley to the marinade for a herby twist.
- BBQ Fun: You can also use a barbecue for an authentic smoky flavor!

SPICY WINGS – THE FIERY FLIERS

Wings & Zings: A spicy twist on the classic, these wings are sure to set your taste buds dancing!

🥣 Serves : 2	🍴 Prep Time : 15 Mins	🕐 Cook Time : 25 Mins

Ingredients:

- 12 chicken wings
- 2 tbsp hot sauce
- 1 tbsp butter, melted
- 1 tsp garlic powder
- Salt to taste
- Vegetable oil for frying

Instructions:

- Marinade Magic: In a bowl, combine hot sauce, melted butter, garlic powder, and salt. Mix well and coat the wings. Marinate for at least 30 minutes.
- Heat & Fry: Heat oil in a deep fryer or large deep skillet to 180°C (355°F). Add chicken wings and fry until golden and crispy.
- Toss & Serve: Once fried, toss the wings in a bit more sauce and serve hot!

Alternatives to Jazz it Up:

- Sweet Heat: Add a splash of honey or maple syrup to the sauce for a sweet and spicy twist.
- Tangy Twist: Squeeze in some lime juice for an added zing

COLESLAW SIDE – CRUNCHY COMPANION

Slaw & Awe: This refreshing side is the perfect complement to your fried favorites.

🥣 Serves : 2	🍴 Prep Time : 15 Mins	🕐 Cook Time : No Cook

Ingredients:

- 200g white cabbage, finely shredded
- 1 carrot, grated
- 1 small red onion, thinly sliced
- 100g mayonnaise
- 1 tbsp cider vinegar
- 1 tsp sugar
- Salt and pepper to taste

Instructions:

- Combine & Coat: In a large bowl, toss together cabbage, carrot, and red onion.
- Dress & Delight: In a separate bowl, whisk together mayonnaise, cider vinegar, sugar, salt, and pepper. Pour this dressing over the vegetables and mix well.
- Chill & Chow: Refrigerate for at least an hour before serving to let flavors meld.

Alternatives to Jazz it Up:

- Fruit Fun: Add some chopped apples or raisins for a sweet bite.
- Creamy Crave: Mix in a dollop of sour cream or Greek yogurt for a creamier texture.

MASHED POTATOES AND GRAVY – SMOOTH OPERATOR

Mash & Splash: Silky mashed potatoes paired with a delightful, rich gravy. Pure, heavenly comfort on a plate!

🥣 Serves : 2	🍴 Prep Time : 15 Mins	🕐 Cook Time : 20 Mins

Ingredients:

- 4 large potatoes, peeled and quartered
- 50g butter
- 100ml milk
- Salt and pepper to taste

For the gravy:

- 2 tbsp butter
- 2 tbsp all-purpose flour
- 500ml chicken or vegetable broth
- 1 tsp onion powder
- 1 tsp garlic powder
- Salt and pepper to taste

Instructions:

- Boil & Soften: In a large pot, cover potatoes with water and bring to a boil. Cook until tender, about 15 minutes.
- Mash & Mix: Drain the potatoes and return them to the pot. Add butter, milk, salt, and pepper. Mash until smooth and creamy.
- Gravy Goodness: In a saucepan, melt butter over medium heat. Stir in flour until smooth and golden. Gradually whisk in the broth, onion powder, and garlic powder. Bring to a boil; cook and stir until thickened. Season with salt and pepper.
- Plate & Pour: Serve your silky mashed potatoes with a generous ladle of gravy on top.

Alternatives to Jazz it Up:

- Cheese Charm: Add grated cheddar or parmesan to your mashed potatoes for an extra layer of flavor.
- Herb Highlight: Finish with a sprinkle of chopped fresh herbs like chives or parsley.

COUSCOUS ROYALE – KINGLY GRAIN GRANDEUR

Fluffy & Filling: Couscous, the iconic grain of North Africa, served with a melody of meats and veggies.

🥣 Serves : 2	🍴 Prep Time : 30 Mins	🕐 Cook Time : 30 Mins

Ingredients:

- 300g couscous
- 300ml chicken stock
- 2 chicken thighs
- 2 lamb sausages
- 2 zucchinis, sliced
- 1 red bell pepper, chopped
- 1 onion, chopped
- 2 tsp Ras el Hanout spice mix
- Fresh cilantro, chopped, for garnish

Instructions:

- Cook & Fluff: In a pot, bring chicken stock to a boil. Remove from heat, add couscous, cover, and let it sit for 5 minutes. Fluff with a fork.
- Sauté & Season: In a separate pan, sauté onion, chicken, sausages, zucchinis, and bell pepper. Season with Ras el Hanout.
- Combine & Garnish: Mix the cooked meat and vegetables with the couscous. Garnish with fresh cilantro.

Alternatives to Jazz it Up:

- Fruity Freshness: Add some pomegranate seeds for a burst of tartness and color.
- Spice Surge: For more heat, add some chopped chili peppers.

MAC 'N' CHEESE DELUXE – CREAMY COMFORT IN A BOWL

American Classic, Tex's Twist: Dive into this creamy concoction where pasta meets cheese in the most delightful manner.

🥣 Serves : 2	🍴 Prep Time : 20 Mins	🕐 Cook Time : 20 Mins

Ingredients:

- 300g elbow macaroni
- 200g cheddar cheese, grated
- 50g parmesan cheese, grated
- 500ml milk
- 50g butter
- 3 tbsp all-purpose flour
- Bread crumbs and parsley for garnish

Instructions:

- Pasta Prep: Cook the elbow macaroni as per package instructions. Drain and set aside.
- Roux Route: In a pan, melt butter and add flour. Cook for a minute before pouring in milk. Stir continuously until thickened.
- Cheese Chorus: Add in the cheddar and parmesan cheese. Stir until you have a smooth cheese sauce.
- Mix & Munch: Combine the pasta and cheese sauce. Transfer to a baking dish, sprinkle bread crumbs on top, and bake at 375°F (190°C) until golden brown. Garnish with parsley.

Alternatives to Jazz it Up:

- Meaty Mix: Add some cooked bacon bits or spicy sausage for an added layer of flavor.
- Veggie Venture: Mix in some steamed broccoli or caramelized onions for a touch of freshness.

CORNBREAD SIDEKICKS - GOLDEN GRAIN GOODNESS

Crispy Corn Companions: These golden morsels are the perfect side to mop up those BBQ sauces and complement your meaty mains.

🥣 Serves : 2	🍴 Prep Time : 15 Mins	⏲ Cook Time : 20 Mins

Ingredients:

- 200g cornmeal
- 100g all-purpose flour
- 250ml buttermilk
- 50g butter, melted
- 1 tbsp sugar
- 1 tsp baking powder
- ½ tsp baking soda

Instructions:

- Mix & Merge: In a bowl, combine cornmeal, flour, sugar, baking powder, and baking soda. Pour in buttermilk and melted butter, and mix until just combined.
- Bake & Bite: Transfer the batter to a greased baking dish and bake at 375°F (190°C) for 20-25 minutes, or until a toothpick comes out clean. Let it cool slightly, then slice and serve.

Alternatives to Jazz it Up:

- Herb Highlight: Add some finely chopped chives or rosemary for an aromatic infusion.
- Cheese Chase: Fold in some grated cheddar or jalapeno slices for a spicier kick.

COLESLAW CRUNCH – CRISP, COOL, & CREAMY

Balancing the BBQ: This crunchy salad provides the perfect counterpoint to your smoky, saucy main dishes.

🥣 Serves : 2	🍴 Prep Time : 15 Mins	🕐 Cook Time : No Cook

Ingredients:

- 200g white cabbage, thinly sliced
- 100g red cabbage, thinly sliced
- 2 carrots, julienned
- 100ml mayonnaise
- 1 tbsp apple cider vinegar
- 1 tsp sugar
- Salt and pepper to taste

Instructions:

- Mix & Marinate: In a large bowl, combine white and red cabbage with julienned carrots.
- Dress & Drench: In a separate bowl, whisk together mayonnaise, apple cider vinegar, sugar, salt, and pepper. Pour this dressing over the vegetables and toss until well coated.
- Chill & Chew: Refrigerate for at least an hour before serving, allowing the flavors to meld.

Alternatives to Jazz it Up:

- Fruit Fusion: Add some finely sliced apple or pineapple chunks for a fruity surprise.
- Nutty Notions: Toss in some roasted pecans or almonds for added crunch and flavor.

CHICKEN FAJITAS – SIZZLING SENSATION

Flavors that Fly: Tender chicken strips with peppers and onions, wrapped in a warm tortilla - this is how you bring the fiesta home.

Serves : 2	Prep Time : 15 Mins	Cook Time : 15 Mins

Ingredients:

- 4 tortillas
- 500g chicken breast, sliced into thin strips
- 1 red bell pepper, julienned
- 1 green bell pepper, julienned
- 1 onion, thinly sliced
- 2 tbsp fajita seasoning
- Olive oil
- Sour cream and salsa for serving

Instructions:

- Sauté & Spice: In a skillet, heat the olive oil. Add the chicken, peppers, and onions. Sauté until chicken is cooked through and vegetables are tender. Sprinkle with fajita seasoning and toss well.
- Wrap & Relish: Warm the tortillas. Place a generous amount of the chicken mixture on each tortilla, fold, and enjoy with sour cream and salsa.

Alternatives to Jazz it Up:

- Cheese Cheer: Sprinkle some grated Monterey Jack or cheddar cheese for a cheesy twist.
- Lime Lift: A squeeze of fresh lime juice brightens up the flavors.

VEGETARIAN QUESADILLAS - CHEESY DELIGHT, NO MEAT IN SIGHT

Folded Flavor: Crispy tortillas encasing a melty cheese and vegetable mix, this is vegetarianism with a zesty twist.

| Serves : 2 | Prep Time : 20 Mins | Cook Time : 10 Mins |

Ingredients:

- 8 tortillas
- 200g cheddar cheese, grated
- 1 red bell pepper, diced
- 1 zucchini, diced
- 1 onion, finely chopped
- Olive oil for frying

Instructions:

- Veggie Venture: In a pan, sauté the peppers, zucchini, and onion until tender.
- Assemble & Cook: Place some of the vegetable mixture and a sprinkle of cheese between two tortillas. Fry in a pan with a bit of olive oil until crispy and golden.

Alternatives to Jazz it Up:

- Mushroom Magic: Add some sautéed mushrooms to the filling for an earthy touch.
- Corn & Bean: Incorporate some cooked corn kernels and black beans for added texture and flavor.

SPICY BEAN BURRITO – WRAPPED WONDER

A Hearty Handful: Flavor-packed beans with fresh veggies all snug in a tortilla, making every bite a fiesta.

🥣 Serves : 2	🍴 Prep Time : 20 Mins	⏲ Cook Time : 15 Mins

Ingredients:

- 4 large tortillas
- 400g canned black beans, drained and rinsed
- 1 onion, finely chopped
- 2 cloves garlic, minced
- 1 jalapeño, finely chopped
- 1 tsp cumin powder
- 50g cheddar cheese, grated
- Salsa, sour cream, and guacamole for serving

Instructions:

- Bean Boost: In a pan, sauté onion, garlic, and jalapeño until softened. Add beans, cumin, and cook until heated through.
- Roll & Relish: Place a generous portion of the bean mixture on a tortilla, sprinkle with cheese, fold the sides in, then roll up tightly. Serve with salsa, sour cream, and guacamole on the side.

Alternatives to Jazz it Up:

- Rice Rise: Add some cooked Mexican rice to the filling for a fuller burrito.
- Veggie Volume: Toss in bell peppers and zucchini for added crunch.

LAMB KOFTA KEBABS – THE DESERT'S DELICACY

Sizzle and Savour: Skewered delights packed with flavors and spices, these kebabs are the stars of any Middle Eastern feast.

Serves : 2   Prep Time : 25 Mins   Cook Time : 15 Mins

Ingredients:

- 500g ground lamb
- 1 small onion, finely chopped
- 2 garlic cloves, minced
- 2 tsp ground cumin
- 2 tsp ground coriander
- 1 tsp smoked paprika
- 1/4 cup fresh parsley, chopped
- 1/4 cup fresh mint, chopped
- Salt and pepper to taste

Instructions:

- Mix & Marinate: In a bowl, combine all ingredients. Mix thoroughly until everything is well incorporated. Let the mixture sit for about an hour for flavors to meld.
- Shape & Skewer: Taking handfuls of the lamb mixture, shape them into elongated kebabs around skewers.
- Grill & Gobble: Grill the kebabs over medium heat, turning occasionally, until they are cooked through and have a nice char on the outside.
- Serve & Satiate: Best served hot with a side of tzatziki or tahini sauce.

Alternatives to Jazz it Up:

- Beef Boost: Try the same recipe with ground beef for a different taste profile.
- Chili Chomp: Add some chopped green chilies to the mix for a fiery kick.

BAKLAVA SWEETS – THE SULTAN'S SWEET ENDINGS

Layers of Love: This sweet pastry made of layers of filo filled with chopped nuts, held together with syrup or honey, is a royal treat!

🥣 Serves : 2	🍴 Prep Time : 30 Mins	🕐 Cook Time : 40 Mins

Ingredients:

- 16 sheets of filo pastry
- 200g mixed nuts (like walnuts, pistachios, and almonds), finely chopped
- 100g melted unsalted butter
- 1 tsp ground cinnamon
- 200g sugar
- 250ml water
- 1 tsp vanilla extract
- Honey for drizzling

Instructions:

- Prep & Layer: Preheat your oven to 180°C. Brush a baking dish with melted butter. Place one sheet of filo at the bottom, brush with more butter, and continue layering until you have 8 sheets layered.
- Nutty Middle: Spread your chopped nuts and sprinkle cinnamon over the filo layers. Then layer the remaining 8 sheets of filo, brushing each with butter as before.
- Slice & Bake: Using a sharp knife, cut the layered pastry into squares or diamond shapes. Bake for about 30-35 minutes or until golden and crisp.
- Syrup Soak: While the baklava bakes, prepare a syrup by boiling sugar and water together until the sugar is dissolved. Add vanilla and let it simmer for 10 minutes. Once the baklava is baked, pour this hot syrup over the pastry.
- Honeyed Finish: Drizzle with honey and let it cool, allowing the syrup to soak in.

Alternatives to Jazz it Up:

- Rose Radiance: Add a splash of rose water to your syrup for a floral note.
- Citrus Charm: A zest of lemon or orange in the nut mixture can add a zingy twist.

SWEDISH MEATBALLS - THE NORSE NOSH

Comfort of the North: Hearty meatballs smothered in a creamy sauce, this dish is what Scandinavian dreams are made of.

Serves : 2   Prep Time : 20 Mins   Cook Time : 25 Mins

Ingredients:

- 500g ground beef
- 100g breadcrumbs
- 1 egg
- 1 small onion, finely chopped
- 200ml beef broth
- 100ml heavy cream
- 2 tbsp butter
- Salt and pepper to taste

Instructions:

- Meatball Mix: Combine ground beef, breadcrumbs, egg, onion, salt, and pepper in a bowl. Shape into small meatballs.
- Golden Brown: In a pan, melt butter and fry meatballs until golden on all sides.
- Creamy Creation: Add beef broth and let it simmer for 10 minutes. Add the heavy cream, let it simmer until the sauce thickens.

Alternatives to Jazz it Up:

- Spice Splendor: Add some grated nutmeg and allspice to the meatball mix for added depth.
- Mushroom Magic: Throw in sliced mushrooms to the sauce for a richer texture.

SMØRREBRØD (OPEN-FACED SANDWICH) – THE DANISH DELIGHT

Bread & Beyond: A slice of rye, topped with whatever your heart desires. It's not just a sandwich, it's a canvas.

Serves : 2 | Prep Time : 15 Mins | Cook Time : No Cook

Ingredients:

- 2 slices of rye bread
- 100g smoked salmon
- Cream cheese
- Fresh dill
- Lemon wedges
- Salt and pepper to taste

Instructions:

- Spread & Layer: Slather the rye bread with a generous amount of cream cheese.
- Top & Garnish: Place smoked salmon on top, sprinkle with fresh dill, salt, and pepper. Serve with a lemon wedge.

Alternatives to Jazz it Up:

- Roast Route: Replace smoked salmon with roast beef slices and horseradish for a hearty variation.
- Veggie Voyage: Layer with roasted veggies and hummus for a vegetarian delight.

SALMON GRAVLAX – THE FJORD'S FAVORITE

Fish & Flavors: Cured to perfection, this salmon dish is Scandinavia on a plate.

Serves : 2	Prep Time : 20 Mins	Cook Time : 36-48 hours

Ingredients:

- 500g fresh salmon fillet, skin on
- 2 tbsp salt
- 2 tbsp sugar
- 1 tbsp crushed black pepper
- Fresh dill, chopped

Instructions:

- Mix & Marinate: Combine salt, sugar, pepper, and dill. Rub this mix onto the salmon fillet.
- Wrap & Wait: Wrap the salmon in cling film and place it in the fridge, with a weight on top, for 48 hours.
- Slice & Serve: Unwrap, scrape off the dill and spices, and slice thinly. Serve with rye bread or crackers.

Alternatives to Jazz it Up:

- Citrus Surge: Add some lemon or orange zest to the curing mix for a fresh twist.
- Beetroot Boost: Introduce grated beetroot in the cure mix for a unique flavor and vibrant color.

CINNAMON BUNS – THE SWEET SWIRLS

Scandinavian Sweets: Soft, fluffy, and swirled with cinnamon goodness, these buns will transport you straight to a cozy Swedish coffee break, known as "fika."

Serves : 2 | Prep Time : 120 Mins | Cook Time : 20 Mins

Ingredients:

- 500g all-purpose flour
- 250ml warm milk
- 75g melted butter
- 75g sugar
- 1 egg
- 2 tsp instant yeast
- Pinch of salt
- For the filling:
- 100g butter, softened
- 50g sugar
- 2 tbsp ground cinnamon

Instructions:

- Dough Delight: In a bowl, mix warm milk, melted butter, and yeast. Let it sit for 10 minutes. Add sugar, egg, and flour. Knead until smooth. Cover and let rise for 1 hour.
- Swirl Setup: Roll out the dough into a large rectangle. Spread softened butter, sprinkle sugar, and ground cinnamon.
- Roll & Cut: Roll the dough tightly from the long edge and cut into 12 slices.
- Bake & Bestow: Place the slices on a baking tray. Let them rise for another 30 minutes. Bake at 180°C (350°F) for 20 minutes or until golden brown.

Alternatives to Jazz it Up:

- Nutty Notion: Add a sprinkle of chopped walnuts or pecans inside the roll for an added crunch.
- Cardamom Care: Incorporate ground cardamom in the dough for a traditional flavor twist.

AEBLESKIVER (DANISH PANCAKE BALLS) – DENMARK'S DELIGHTFUL DOTS

Ball-shaped Bliss: Dive into these light and fluffy pancake balls, often found at Christmas markets, but why wait for December?

Serves : 2	Prep Time : 15 Mins	Cook Time : 20 Mins

Ingredients:

- 250g all-purpose flour
- 2 tsp sugar
- 1/2 tsp baking soda
- 1/2 tsp salt
- 2 eggs, separated
- 500ml buttermilk
- Butter for frying

Instructions:

- Batter Basics: In a bowl, mix flour, sugar, baking soda, and salt. Add egg yolks and buttermilk, mixing until smooth. In another bowl, beat egg whites until stiff peaks form. Fold them gently into the batter.
- Frying Fun: Heat up an aebleskiver pan. Add a small amount of butter into each hole. Pour the batter into each hole until 2/3 full.
- Flip & Feast: As they cook, use a skewer to turn them to ensure even cooking. Cook until golden brown. Serve with powdered sugar and jam.

Alternatives to Jazz it Up:

- Fruity Fill: Add a small dollop of apple sauce or jam in the center for a fruity surprise.
- Chocolate Charm: A piece of chocolate in the center will melt and give you a gooey core.

KOSHARI (RICE AND LENTILS) - CAIRO'S COMFORT CUISINE

Layers of Delight: This popular Egyptian street food combines rice, pasta, lentils, and tomato sauce, giving a flavorful and fulfilling meal.

🥣 Serves : 2   🍴 Prep Time : 25 Mins   ⏱ Cook Time : 40 Mins

Ingredients:

- 100g rice
- 100g brown lentils
- 100g macaroni
- 1 large onion, finely sliced
- 2 cloves garlic, minced
- 400g canned tomatoes
- 2 tbsp vinegar
- 1 tsp cumin
- Salt, pepper, and chili to taste
- Vegetable oil for frying

Instructions:

- Layered Cooking: Boil the rice, lentils, and macaroni separately until each is cooked. Drain and set aside.
- Crispy Onions: Fry the sliced onions in vegetable oil until they turn crispy and golden. Set some aside for garnishing.
- Spicy Sauce: In the same pan, add garlic, tomatoes, vinegar, cumin, salt, pepper, and chili. Let simmer until you have a rich sauce.
- Mix & Serve: In a serving dish, layer rice, lentils, and macaroni. Pour the spicy sauce over and garnish with the crispy onions.

Alternatives to Jazz it Up:

- Protein Punch: Add some cooked chickpeas for an added layer of flavor and nutrition.
- Fresh Finish: Garnish with fresh parsley or coriander for a burst of color and freshness.

HARIRA (TOMATO AND LENTIL SOUP) – MEDINA'S WARM EMBRACE

Hearty & Wholesome: This nourishing soup, often used to break the Ramadan fast, is full of flavors and textures.

🥣 Serves : 2	🍴 Prep Time : 20 Mins	🕐 Cook Time : 40 Mins

Ingredients:

- 150g lentils, soaked overnight
- 2 tomatoes, chopped
- 1 onion, chopped
- 2 celery stalks, chopped
- 1 tsp ground cumin
- 1 tsp ground turmeric
- 1 tsp ground ginger
- 500ml chicken stock
- Fresh cilantro and parsley, chopped

Instructions:

- Sauté & Spice: In a pot, sauté onion and celery until soft. Add spices and stir until aromatic.
- Simmer & Serve: Add lentils, tomatoes, and chicken stock. Simmer for 30-40 minutes, until lentils are tender. Stir in fresh herbs just before serving.

Alternatives to Jazz it Up:

- Meaty Moment: Add some shredded chicken or lamb for a more robust version.
- Lemon Lift: Serve with a wedge of lemon for a zesty kick.

MINT TEA AND MA'AMOUL (DATE FILLED COOKIES) – SWEET SOUK SOIREE

Refreshing & Rich: The perfect end to a Moroccan meal - aromatic mint tea paired with date-filled delights.

🥣 Serves : 2	🍴 Prep Time : 20 Mins	⏲ Cook Time : 15 Mins

Ingredients:

- Fresh mint leaves
- 1 tbsp green tea leaves
- Sugar to taste
- For the Ma'amoul:
- 200g all-purpose flour
- 100g butter, melted
- 50g powdered sugar
- 100g dates, pitted and finely chopped
- 1 tsp orange blossom water

Instructions:

- For the Tea:
- Brew & Serve: In a teapot, place fresh mint, green tea leaves, and sugar. Pour boiling water and let steep for 5 minutes. Pour into glasses and serve.
- For the Ma'amoul:
- Mix & Fill: Combine flour, butter, and sugar. Take small amounts of dough, flatten, place some chopped dates in the center, then close and shape into a ball.
- Bake & Enjoy: Place on a baking sheet and bake at 180°C for 15-20 minutes, until slightly golden. Let cool and enjoy with the mint tea.

Alternatives to Jazz it Up:

- Nutty Nibble: Add some finely chopped walnuts or pistachios to the date filling.
- Spice Sprinkle: Dust the cookies with a mix of powdered sugar and cinnamon.

CUBAN SANDWICH – ISLANDER'S ICONIC BITE

Layered & Luscious: The ultimate meaty sandwich, packed with flavors and pressed to perfection.

🥣 Serves : 2	🍴 Prep Time : 15 Mins	⏱ Cook Time : 10 Mins

Ingredients:

- 2 long rolls, split
- 200g roast pork, sliced
- 100g ham, sliced
- 50g Swiss cheese, sliced
- 4 pickles, sliced
- Mustard
- Butter for spreading

Instructions:

- Layer & Press: Spread mustard on one side of each roll. Layer with ham, pork, cheese, and pickles. Close the sandwiches.
- Grill & Serve: Butter the outside of the sandwiches. Press and grill in a sandwich press or skillet until crispy and golden. Slice diagonally and serve.

Alternatives to Jazz it Up:

- Spicy Slather: Add some hot sauce or jalapeños for a fiery twist.
- Veggie Variation: Replace meats with grilled zucchinis and eggplants for a vegetarian treat.

ROPA VIEJA (SHREDDED BEEF STEW) – HAVANA'S HEARTY HUG

Rustic & Robust: Slow-cooked beef, transformed into a fragrant and flavorful stew.

🥣 Serves : 2	🍴 Prep Time : 30 Mins	🕐 Cook Time : 2.5 hours

Ingredients:

- 500g beef flank steak
- 1 onion, sliced
- 1 bell pepper, sliced
- 3 garlic cloves, minced
- 1 can diced tomatoes
- 1 tsp cumin
- 1 tsp paprika
- 2 bay leaves
- Salt and pepper to taste

Instructions:

- Sear & Simmer: In a pot, sear the beef on all sides. Add all the other ingredients and enough water to cover the beef.
- Shred & Serve: Cook on low for 4-6 hours until the beef is tender. Shred the beef in the pot using two forks. Adjust seasoning and serve over rice.

Alternatives to Jazz it Up:

- Olive Offer: Stir in some green olives for a salty and tangy contrast.
- Wine Wonder: Replace half the water with red wine for deeper flavor.

ARROZ CON POLLO (CHICKEN AND RICE) – CUBAN COMFORT CLASSIC

Golden & Gratifying: A simple yet soul-satisfying dish that showcases the magic of chicken and rice cooked together.

🥣 Serves : 2	🍴 Prep Time : 25 Mins	🕐 Cook Time : 45 Mins

Ingredients:

- 4 chicken thighs
- 200g rice
- 1 onion, chopped
- 1 bell pepper, chopped
- 2 garlic cloves, minced
- 1 tsp turmeric or saffron for color
- 500ml chicken stock
- Salt and pepper to taste

Instructions:

- Brown & Set: In a pot, brown the chicken thighs on both sides. Remove and set aside.
- Sauté & Simmer: In the same pot, sauté onion, bell pepper, and garlic. Add rice and stir until grains are well-coated. Return chicken to the pot, add turmeric, stock, salt, and pepper.
- Cook & Serve: Cover and simmer for 20-25 minutes, until rice is cooked and chicken is tender. Serve hot.

Alternatives to Jazz it Up:

- Peas Pleaser: Stir in some green peas towards the end for color and freshness.
- Tomato Twist: Add diced tomatoes to the rice for added tang and color.

BLACK BEAN SOUP – CARIBBEAN CAULDRON

Deep & Delightful: A rich and flavorful bean soup that warms the heart and soothes the soul.

🥣 Serves : 2	🍴 Prep Time : 20 Mins	⏱️ Cook Time : 120 Mins

Ingredients:

- 200g dried black beans, soaked overnight
- 1 onion, chopped
- 2 garlic cloves, minced
- 1 bell pepper, chopped
- 1 tsp cumin
- 500ml chicken or vegetable stock
- Salt and pepper to taste

Instructions:

- Sauté & Simmer: In a pot, sauté onion, garlic, and bell pepper until soft. Add soaked beans, cumin, stock, salt, and pepper.
- Blend & Boil: Cook until beans are tender. For a thicker consistency, blend part of the soup and return to the pot. Boil for another 5 minutes.

Alternatives to Jazz it Up:

- Zesty Zing: Serve with lime wedges for a squeeze of freshness.
- Creamy Contrasts: Top with a dollop of sour cream and fresh cilantro.

TANDOORI ROTI – THE RUSTIC ROUNDEL

Taste the Tradition: This classic Indian bread brings the essence of tandoor (clay oven) right to your dinner plate.

Serves : 2   Prep Time : 5 Mins   Cook Time : 30 Mins

Ingredients:

- 2 cups whole wheat flour
- Water, as required to knead the dough
- A pinch of salt
- Butter or ghee for brushing

Instructions:

- Doughy Delight: In a mixing bowl, combine the whole wheat flour and salt. Gradually add water and knead to form a soft and pliable dough. Cover with a damp cloth and let it rest for 30 minutes.
- Roll & Rise: Divide the dough into 8 equal parts. Roll each part into a ball and then roll it out into a circle using a rolling pin.
- Tandoori Twist: Place a tava (griddle) on high heat. Once hot, put the rolled roti on it. When bubbles start to appear, flip the roti and cook the other side. Using tongs, expose the roti directly to the flame until it puffs up and gets those lovely charred spots.
- Butter Bliss: Brush with butter or ghee while still hot and serve immediately.

Alternatives to Jazz it Up:

- Herby Hand: Sprinkle some chopped garlic and coriander leaves on the roti before cooking for a garlic-flavored version.
- Sesame Spin: Sprinkle some white sesame seeds on the rolled dough for added texture and flavor.

MARGHERITA PIZZA – THE QUEEN OF PIZZAS

Naples' Neapolitan Gem: Simplicity meets flavor in this timeless classic. Crispy crust, melted cheese, fresh tomatoes - perfection!

🍲 Serves : 2	✗ Prep Time : 20 Mins	🕐 Cook Time : 15 Mins

Ingredients:

- 1 pizza dough (store-bought or homemade)
- 1 cup mozzarella cheese, shredded
- 2 tomatoes, thinly sliced
- Fresh basil leaves
- 2 tbsp olive oil
- 1 tsp dried oregano
- Salt to taste

Instructions:

- Preheat Passion: Start by preheating your oven to 250°C (480°F).
- Dough Dynamics: Roll out your pizza dough on a floured surface, stretching it to your desired thickness.
- Topping Time: Place it on a pizza stone or baking sheet. Brush it with olive oil, and then lay out the tomato slices evenly. Sprinkle the shredded mozzarella, and season with salt and oregano.
- Baking Bliss: Slide it into the oven and bake for about 10-12 minutes or until the edges are golden brown and the cheese is bubbling with joy.
- Fresh Finale: Once out of the oven, adorn with fresh basil leaves. Slice, serve, and savour!

Alternatives to Jazz it Up:

- Cheese Cheer: Add dollops of ricotta for an extra cheesy punch.
- Chili Charm: Sprinkle red chili flakes for some heat.

TOMATO BRUSCHETTA - TUSCANY'S TOASTED TREAT

Renaissance Refreshment: Crunchy bread meets juicy tomatoes in this timeless appetizer. A bite into Italian summer!

Serves : 2   **Prep Time : 10 Mins**   **Cook Time : 5 Mins**

Ingredients:

- 1 French baguette, sliced
- 3 ripe tomatoes, diced
- 3 garlic cloves, minced (keep 1 clove whole for rubbing)
- Handful of fresh basil, chopped
- 2 tbsp extra virgin olive oil, plus extra for brushing
- Salt and freshly ground black pepper to taste

Instructions:

- Bread Basics: Preheat your oven to 200°C (390°F). Arrange the baguette slices on a baking sheet, brush lightly with olive oil, and toast for about 5 minutes, or until golden and crispy.
- Tomato Topping: In a mixing bowl, combine the diced tomatoes, minced garlic, chopped basil, olive oil, salt, and pepper. Mix well, letting the flavors marry.
- Garlic Goodness: Once your bread is toasted and cooled slightly, rub each slice with the whole garlic clove. This imparts a beautiful, subtle garlic aroma.
- Mount & Munch: Spoon generous amounts of the tomato mixture onto each slice. Serve immediately and enjoy the crunch!

Alternatives to Jazz it Up:

- Cheesy Charm: Add a slice of fresh mozzarella beneath the tomato mix for a creamy delight.
- Balsamic Boost: Drizzle a little aged balsamic vinegar for an added depth of flavor.

TIRAMISU DELIGHT - VENICE'S VELVETY DESSERT

Canal-Side Creaminess: Indulge in layers of coffee-soaked ladyfingers and rich mascarpone. It's Italy's sweet embrace!

🥣 Serves : 2	🍴 Prep Time : 30 Mins	🕐 Cook Time : No Cook

Ingredients:

- 200g ladyfingers
- 250g mascarpone cheese
- 3 large egg yolks
- 75g granulated sugar
- 300ml strong brewed coffee, cooled
- 2 tbsp coffee liqueur (optional)
- Unsweetened cocoa powder for dusting
- 1 tsp vanilla extract

Instructions:

- Egg Emulsion: In a bowl, whisk together the egg yolks and sugar until pale and creamy. Add the mascarpone cheese and vanilla extract, mixing until smooth and well combined.
- Coffee Cocktail: In a separate dish, combine the brewed coffee with the coffee liqueur.
- Layering Luxury: Dip the ladyfingers briefly into the coffee mixture, ensuring they're soaked but not soggy. Arrange a layer at the bottom of your serving dish. Spread a layer of the mascarpone mixture over the ladyfingers. Repeat layers until all ingredients are used up, finishing with a mascarpone layer.
- Dusty Delight: Using a sieve, sprinkle the top layer with unsweetened cocoa powder.
- Chill & Cherish: Refrigerate for at least 4 hours or, ideally, overnight to let the flavors meld. Dig in and drift into Venetian dreams!

Alternatives to Jazz it Up:

- Chocolate Chunks: Add chocolate chips or shaved chocolate between layers for added indulgence.
- Berry Burst: Top with fresh strawberries or raspberries before serving for a fruity touch.

ORIGINAL RECIPE CHICKEN - THE ICONIC CRISP

Cluckin' Classic: The star of the show! This legendary recipe brings the crispy, juicy joy without the queue.

Serves : 2   Prep Time : 20 Mins   Cook Time : 40 Mins

Ingredients:

- 8 pieces chicken (mixture of thighs, drumsticks, wings)
- 200g all-purpose flour
- 2 tsp salt
- 1 tsp white pepper
- 1 tsp smoked paprika
- 1 tsp onion powder
- 1 tsp garlic powder
- 1/2 tsp cayenne pepper
- 250ml buttermilk
- Vegetable oil for frying

Instructions:

- Marinate & Mingle: In a bowl, soak the chicken pieces in buttermilk for at least 1 hour (overnight is even better).
- Mix & Match: In a large mixing bowl, combine flour, salt, and all your spices. This is the magical mix!
- Dredge & Dip: Remove each chicken piece from the buttermilk, letting excess drip off. Coat them generously in the flour mixture.
- Fry & Feast: In a large skillet, heat the oil to 175°C (350°F). Carefully place chicken pieces in. Fry until golden brown and cooked through, turning occasionally. Drain on kitchen paper.

Alternatives to Jazz it Up:

- Zesty Zing: Add some lemon zest to your flour mixture for a citrusy kick.
- Herb Haven: Incorporate some dried thyme and rosemary for an herby touch.

SODA BREAD SANDWICH - DUBLIN'S DAILY DELIGHT

Bread, the Irish Way: Forget the regular slices; this is bread with an Irish twist. Load it up with your favorite fillings and get a bite of Ireland!

🥣 Serves : 2	🍴 Prep Time : 15 Mins	⏲ Cook Time : 40 Mins

Ingredients:

- 4 slices of soda bread
- 100g smoked salmon
- 1 tbsp cream cheese
- 1 tsp dill, chopped
- Squeeze of lemon juice
- Salt and pepper to taste

Instructions:

- Soda Setup: Toast the soda bread slices until they're slightly crispy but still soft inside.
- Salmon Spread: Mix the smoked salmon with cream cheese, dill, lemon juice, salt, and pepper.
- Sandwich & Serve: Generously spread the salmon mixture between two slices of the soda bread, creating a sandwich. Enjoy with a cup of tea and daydream of the Irish coastline!

Alternatives to Jazz it Up:

- Egg-cellent: Add a sliced boiled egg for extra protein.
- Veggie Variant: For a vegetarian option, replace smoked salmon with sliced cucumber and radish.

BANGERS AND MASH - THE DUBLIN DUET

Pub Classic at Home: Sausages and mashed potatoes, a duet as iconic as any. No need to stroll to the local pub when you can cook up this comfort right at home!

Serves : 2   Prep Time : 20 Mins   Cook Time : 30 Mins

Ingredients:

- 8 pork sausages
- 4 large potatoes, peeled and quartered
- 50g butter
- 100ml milk
- Salt and pepper to taste
- 1 onion, thinly sliced
- 2 tbsp oil
- 300ml beef broth
- 1 tbsp flour
- 1 tsp Worcestershire sauce

Instructions:

- Banger Bliss: In a frying pan, heat the oil and fry your sausages until they're browned all over and cooked through. Set them aside, keeping them warm.
- Mash Magic: Boil the potatoes until tender. Drain and mash them with butter and milk. Season with salt and pepper. Whip it until it's creamy.
- Onion Odyssey: Using the same frying pan, add a bit more oil if needed, and fry the onions until they are soft and golden.
- Gravy Goals: Sprinkle flour over the onions and stir for a minute. Slowly add in the beef broth and Worcestershire sauce. Let it simmer until it thickens to a rich gravy. Season to taste.
- Plate & Praise: On a plate, place a generous dollop of mash, top with sausages, and drizzle the onion gravy over. Dive into the ultimate comfort food!

Alternatives to Jazz it Up:

- Herb Hints: Add some chopped rosemary or thyme into the mash for an aromatic twist.
- Spicy Spin: Toss in a pinch of cayenne or some chili flakes into the gravy for a bit of a kick.

VEGETARIAN POTSTICKERS - PAN-FRIED PERFECTION

Sticker than the Rest: No more store-bought dumplings when you can stick to these homemade delights. A perfect bite every time!

| 🥣 Serves : 4 | 🍴 Prep Time : 30 Mins | 🕐 Cook Time : 10 Mins |

Ingredients:

- 20 dumpling wrappers
- 50g shredded cabbage
- 50g grated carrot
- 2 spring onions, finely chopped
- 1 tablespoon soy sauce
- 1 teaspoon sesame oil
- Oil for frying
- Water for steaming

Instructions:

- Filling Fiesta: In a mixing bowl, combine cabbage, carrot, spring onions, soy sauce, and sesame oil. Mix until everything is well combined.
- Wrap & Roll: Lay out a dumpling wrapper, place a spoonful of your filling in the centre, wet the edges, fold, and press to seal.
- Pan-fried Magic: In a non-stick pan with a lid, heat a little oil. Place your potstickers in, flat side down. Once the bottoms are golden, pour a splash of water and quickly cover with the lid. Let them steam until the water has evaporated and they're tender to the bite.

Alternatives to Jazz it Up:

- Dip & Dive: Serve with a spicy sriracha mayo or classic soy dipping sauce.
- Fillings Galore: Swap out veggies for minced chicken, pork, or prawn.

CLASSIC CALIFORNIA ROLL – THE SUSHI STALWART

Embrace the Roll: A fusion of East meets West, this roll is a love letter from California to Japan. A perfect start to your sushi-making saga.

Serves : 2	Prep Time : 30 Mins	Cook Time : No Cook

Ingredients:

- 2 nori sheets
- 200g sushi rice, cooked and seasoned
- 50g crab stick or imitation crab
- 50g ripe avocado, thinly sliced
- 30g cucumber, julienned
- Sesame seeds and soy sauce, for serving

Instructions:

- Mat Magic: Place the nori on your sushi mat, shiny side down. Wet your fingers (to prevent sticking) and spread an even layer of sushi rice over the nori.
- Filling Fun: Lay your crab sticks, avocado slices, and cucumber juliennes neatly across the center of the rice.
- Roll & Reveal: Carefully lift the edge of your mat closest to you, and roll tightly but gently. Slice with a damp knife into 8 even pieces.
- Serve & Savor: Plate up with a sprinkle of sesame seeds and a dip into your favorite soy sauce.

Alternatives to Jazz it Up:

- Spice Sprinkle: Add a dash of spicy mayo or wasabi for that extra kick.
- Topping Trade: Fancy some shrimp or tuna? Lay it atop your roll for a delicious variation.

CLASSIC BEEF TACOS – TIMELESS TASTE TRIUMPH

Savor the Sizzle: Crispy taco shells embracing spiced beef and fresh toppings - a bite of Mexican tradition.

🥣 Serves : 2	🍴 Prep Time : 20 Mins	⏲ Cook Time : 10 Mins

Ingredients:

- 8 taco shells
- 500g ground beef
- 1 taco seasoning mix
- 50g cheddar cheese, grated
- 1 tomato, diced
- 1 onion, finely chopped
- Lettuce, shredded
- Sour cream for serving

Instructions:

- Beefy Beginnings: In a pan, cook the ground beef until browned. Add the taco seasoning and mix well.
- Assemble & Attack: Fill each taco shell with the beef mixture, then top with cheese, tomatoes, onions, and lettuce. Drizzle with sour cream.

Alternatives to Jazz it Up:

- Heat Hike: Add some jalapeños for an extra kick.
- Guacamole Glory: A dollop of fresh guacamole takes these tacos to another level.

SHRIMP TEMPURA UDON - NOODLE NIRVANA

Whisked Away to Osaka: Dive into a bowl where crispy tempura meets velvety noodles, all bathed in a soothing broth that warms the soul.

🥣 Serves : 2	🍴 Prep Time : 20 Mins	⏱ Cook Time : 20 Mins

Ingredients:

- 150g udon noodles
- 6 large shrimps, peeled and deveined
- 100g tempura batter
- 750ml dashi broth
- 2 tbsp soy sauce
- 1 tbsp mirin
- Oil for frying
- Sliced green onions and nori for garnish

Instructions:

- Broth Basics: In a pot, simmer the dashi broth with soy sauce and mirin. Keep warm.
- Tempura Triumph: Heat the oil in a deep pan. Dip the shrimps into the tempura batter and fry until golden. Drain on paper towels.
- Noodle Nest: Cook the udon noodles as per package instructions, then divide them between two bowls.
- Assemble & Admire: Pour the warm broth over the noodles, top with tempura shrimps, and garnish with green onions and nori.

Alternatives to Jazz it Up:

- Veggie Volume: Add some tempura veggies like bell peppers or zucchini for a delightful crunch.
- Tofu Twist: For a vegetarian alternative, swap the shrimp for crispy tempura tofu cubes.

MISO SOUP – SIP OF SERENITY

Whisked Away to Osaka: Dive into a bowl where crispy tempura meets velvety noodles, all bathed in a soothing broth that warms the soul.

Serves : 2 | Prep Time : 10 Mins | Cook Time : 15 Mins

Ingredients:

- 500ml dashi broth
- 2 tbsp miso paste
- 50g tofu, cubed
- 1 green onion, finely chopped
- 1 small sheet nori, cut into strips

Instructions:

- Broth Beginnings: In a pot, heat the dashi broth but avoid bringing it to a boil.
- Miso Mix: In a separate bowl, mix a little hot dashi broth with the miso paste to make a smooth mixture. Add this back to the pot.
- Tofu Tumble: Add the tofu cubes and simmer gently for a couple of minutes.
- Serve & Savor: Pour the soup into bowls, top with green onions and nori strips.

Alternatives to Jazz it Up:

- Mushroom Magic: Add some sliced shiitake mushrooms for an earthy flavor and texture contrast.
- Seaweed Surge: Introduce wakame seaweed for an additional depth of flavor and a delightful chewy texture.

TERIYAKI CHICKEN BOWL – TOKYO'S TANTALIZING TREASURE

Feast on Flavor: A bowlful of joy, fragrant rice is crowned with glistening teriyaki chicken, delivering a delectable bite that dances between sweet and savory.

🥣 Serves : 2	🍴 Prep Time : 20 Mins	⏱ Cook Time : 20 Mins

Ingredients:

- 200g boneless chicken thighs, cubed
- 300g cooked jasmine or sushi rice
- 50ml teriyaki sauce (store-bought or homemade)
- 1 tbsp sesame oil
- 1 green onion, finely sliced
- Toasted sesame seeds for garnish

Instructions:

- Sear & Sizzle: In a hot pan with sesame oil, sear the chicken pieces until browned.
- Teriyaki Turn: Pour the teriyaki sauce over the chicken and let it simmer until the chicken is cooked through and the sauce thickens.
- Bowl & Build: Place a serving of rice in each bowl. Top with teriyaki chicken, and garnish with green onions and toasted sesame seeds.

Alternatives to Jazz it Up:

- Veggie Venture: Add some steamed broccoli or bell pepper strips for added color and nutrition.
- Spicy Surge: Drizzle a bit of sriracha or sprinkle some red pepper flakes for a fiery kick.

CHURROS WITH CHOCOLATE DIP – SWEET, SUGARY SERENADE

Crispy & Creamy: These golden sticks of joy, dusted with sugar and cinnamon, paired with a velvety chocolate dip, are the perfect end to your Mexican feast.

Serves : 2 | **Prep Time : 20 Mins** | **Cook Time : 15 Mins**

Ingredients:

- 200g all-purpose flour
- 250ml water
- 50g unsalted butter
- A pinch of salt
- 50g sugar
- 1 tsp cinnamon powder
- Oil for frying
- 100g dark chocolate
- 150ml heavy cream

Instructions:

- Dough Dream: In a pot, bring water, butter, and salt to a boil. Remove from heat, and stir in the flour until a dough forms. Allow to cool.
- Fry & Flavor: Heat oil in a deep pan. Pipe or shape the dough into long sticks and fry until golden. Mix sugar and cinnamon and roll the hot churros in this mix.
- Chocolate Charm: Melt the chocolate in a bowl. Heat the cream just until warm and mix with the chocolate to form a smooth dip.
- Dip & Devour: Serve the churros hot with the chocolate dip on the side.

Alternatives to Jazz it Up:

- Zesty Zeal: Add some orange zest to the chocolate dip for a citrusy punch.
- Caramel Core: Fill the inside of the churros with caramel sauce for a gooey surprise.

CROQUE MONSIEUR – THE ELEGANT GRILLED CHEESE

Ooh La La: This is not just a sandwich; it's an experience! Creamy bechamel, ham, and melted cheese make this a French favorite.

Serves : 2	Prep Time : 10 Mins	Cook Time : 20 Mins

Ingredients:

- 4 slices of white bread
- 100g ham slices
- 100g Gruyère cheese, grated
- 50g butter
- 50g flour
- 500ml milk

Instructions:

- Bechamel Bliss: Melt butter in a saucepan, stir in the flour and cook for 2 minutes. Gradually whisk in milk, cooking until the sauce thickens. Season and set aside.
- Sandwich Setup: On one slice of bread, layer ham, a sprinkle of cheese, and some bechamel. Top with another slice. Do the same for the other sandwich.
- Golden Grilled: In a hot skillet, melt some butter. Place the sandwich, ensuring both sides are golden and the cheese is melted.

Alternatives to Jazz it Up:

- Mademoiselle Touch: Add a fried egg on top, and you have a Croque Mademoiselle!
- Veggie Venture: Swap the ham for sautéed mushrooms and spinach.

VEGGIE DELIGHT SUB – GREEN & GORGEOUS

Veg Out: Loaded with fresh, crispy vegetables, this sub is a crunchy and colorful delight.

Serves : 2   Prep Time : 10 Mins   Cook Time : No Cook

Ingredients:

- 2 sub rolls, split
- 2 lettuce leaves, shredded
- 1 tomato, thinly sliced
- 1 cucumber, thinly sliced
- 1 red bell pepper, julienned
- 1/4 red onion, thinly sliced
- 2 tbsp mayonnaise or vegan mayo
- Salt and pepper to taste

Instructions:

- Layer & Load: Start by spreading a tablespoon of mayo on each roll. Then, layer on the lettuce, tomato slices, cucumber slices, bell pepper, and red onion.
- Season & Serve: Sprinkle with salt and pepper to taste. Close up your sub and dig in!

Alternatives to Jazz it Up:

- Spread Spectrum: Swap mayo for hummus, guacamole, or tzatziki for a flavor twist.
- Cheese Choice: Add slices of your favorite cheese or vegan cheese for extra creaminess.

ULTIMATE MEAT FEAST – MEATY MARVEL

Meat Mountain: This sub is a carnivore's dream, stacked high with a variety of meats.

🥣 Serves : 2	🍴 Prep Time : 15 Mins	⏰ Cook Time : 10 Mins

Ingredients:

- 2 sub rolls, split
- 4 slices ham
- 4 slices roast beef
- 4 slices turkey
- 2 slices swiss cheese
- 2 slices cheddar cheese
- 4 slices of bacon, cooked crisp
- Lettuce, tomato, and red onion for garnish
- 2 tbsp mustard or mayo
- Salt and pepper to taste

Instructions:

- Meat Medley: On the bottom half of each roll, layer ham, roast beef, turkey, swiss cheese, cheddar cheese, and crispy bacon.
- Garnish & Go: Top with lettuce, tomato, and red onion. Spread mustard or mayo on the top half of the roll, season with salt and pepper, and close up your sub.
- Devour & Dream: Bite into this meaty marvel and experience a meat lover's paradise.

Alternatives to Jazz it Up:

- Sauce Swap: Use BBQ sauce, ranch dressing, or horseradish sauce for a different flavor profile.
- Green Gourmet: Add some sliced avocados or pickles for extra texture and flavor.

CHICKEN PESTO MELT – ITALIAN ELEGANCE

Pesto Perfection: Succulent chicken, aromatic pesto, and melting cheese unite in this Italian-inspired sub masterpiece.

Serves : 2   Prep Time : 15 Mins   Cook Time : 10 Mins

Ingredients:

- 2 sub rolls, split
- 2 chicken breasts, grilled and thinly sliced
- 3 tbsp pesto sauce
- 4 slices of mozzarella cheese
- A handful of fresh basil leaves
- 1 tomato, sliced
- Salt and pepper to taste

Instructions:

- Pesto Pleasure: Begin by spreading a generous layer of pesto sauce on the insides of your sub rolls.
- Chicken & Cheese: On the bottom half, lay out your sliced grilled chicken. Top this with slices of mozzarella cheese.
- Basil & Balance: Scatter a few fresh basil leaves and slices of tomato over the chicken and cheese. Season with a touch of salt and pepper.
- Heat & Melt: If you desire a warmer sub, pop your assembled subs (open-faced) under a grill or in an oven just until the cheese begins to melt.
- Serve & Savor: Close up your sub rolls and delve into the flavors of Italy without leaving your kitchen!

Alternatives to Jazz it Up:

- Red Rhapsody: Drizzle some sun-dried tomato oil or add slices of sun-dried tomato for an intensified tomato flavor.
- Zingy Zest: Add a sprinkle of chili flakes for a slight kick or some lemon zest for a fresh twist.

CLASSIC CHICKEN TIKKA MASALA – THE CROWN JEWEL

Masala Magic: This creamy, tomatoey delight is the reigning monarch of Indian curries worldwide.

🥣 Serves : 2	🍴 Prep Time : 25 Mins	🕐 Cook Time : 40 Mins

Ingredients:

- 4 chicken breasts, diced
- 2 onions, finely chopped
- 3 garlic cloves, minced
- 1 inch ginger, grated
- 2 tbsp tomato puree
- 200ml heavy cream
- 2 tbsp tikka masala spice mix (store-bought for convenience)
- 2 tbsp oil
- Fresh coriander for garnish
- Salt to taste

Instructions:

- Fry & Aroma Rise: In a pan, heat the oil and sauté the onions until translucent. Add in the garlic and ginger, and fry until aromatic.
- Chicken Dive: Introduce the diced chicken and cook until it's slightly browned all over.
- Spice & Sauce Surprise: Stir in the tikka masala spice mix and the tomato puree. Mix well, ensuring the chicken is thoroughly coated.
- Cream Dream: Pour in the heavy cream, give it a good mix and let it simmer for about 15 minutes until the chicken is tender and the sauce is thick and creamy.
- Garnish & Relish: Season with salt, garnish with fresh coriander, and serve hot with rice or bread.

Alternatives to Jazz it Up:

- Veggie Venture: Replace chicken with mushrooms or tofu for a vegetarian twist.
- Heat Heat: Spice it up by adding fresh chopped green chillies or red chilli powder to your desired heat level.

SPICY PERI-PERI PRAWNS – OCEAN'S FIERY KISS

A Sizzling Sea Breeze: Who needs the beach when you can have a spicy ocean party on your plate? Prep those prawns and let's ride the spicy wave!

🥣 Serves : 4	🍴 Prep Time : 15 Mins	⏱ Cook Time : 10 Mins

Ingredients:

- 300g fresh prawns, deveined and shelled
- 3 tablespoons peri-peri sauce
- 1 tablespoon garlic, finely minced
- 1 tablespoon olive oil
- Freshly chopped parsley for garnish
- Lemon wedges for serving

Instructions:

- Prawn Prep: Ensure all prawns are cleaned, shelled, and deveined. Lay them out on a paper towel to pat dry.
- Saucy Soak: In a mixing bowl, merge the peri-peri sauce, minced garlic, and olive oil. Tumble the prawns into this mix, making sure they get a good spicy coat. Allow them to marinate for about 20 minutes.
- Heat & Eat: Light up a skillet over medium heat. Once it's ready for action, lay your prawns in. Let them sizzle for about 2 minutes each side, or until they're blushing pink.
- Final Flourish: Slide those prawns onto a plate, shower them with chopped parsley, and present with lemon wedges. A squeeze of lemon, and you're diving deep into the spicy ocean!

Alternatives to Jazz it Up:

- Zesty Zing: Grate some lemon zest into the marinade for an extra citrus punch.
- Chilli Challenge: Add a finely chopped red chilli to the marinade for an additional heat kick.
- Grilled Glory: Instead of the skillet, throw them on a grill for that smoky char.

SOUVLAKI SKEWERS - GRECIAN GRILLED GLORY

Fire & Flavor: Succulent meat, marinated to perfection, and grilled to capture the essence of Greek summer evenings.

🥣 Serves : 2	🍴 Prep Time : 20 Mins	🕐 Cook Time : 15 Mins

Ingredients:

- 500g chicken, pork, or lamb, cut into chunks
- 3 garlic cloves, minced
- Juice of 1 lemon
- 2 tbsp olive oil
- 1 tsp dried oregano
- Salt & pepper to taste

Instructions:

- Marinate & Wait: In a bowl, mix garlic, lemon juice, olive oil, oregano, salt, and pepper. Add meat chunks, ensuring they're well coated. Marinate for at least 2 hours or overnight.
- Skewer & Grill: Thread the meat onto skewers. Grill on a barbecue or grill pan for 10-12 minutes, turning occasionally until golden and cooked through.
- Serve & Savor: Serve hot with tzatziki sauce and a side of pita bread. Garnish with fresh lemon wedges.

Alternatives to Jazz it Up:

- Veggie Verve: Use halloumi cheese or mushrooms instead of meat for a vegetarian version.
- Herb Enhance: Mix in fresh rosemary or thyme into the marinade for an aromatic twist.

TZATZIKI WITH PITA BREAD – AEGEAN'S APPETIZING APERITIF

Cool & Creamy: Dive into this refreshing yogurt-based dip, accentuated by the crisp bite of cucumber and the warmth of garlic.

🥣 **Serves : 2**   🍴 **Prep Time : 15 Mins**   ⏱ **Cook Time : No Cook**

Ingredients:

- 250g Greek yogurt
- 1 medium cucumber, finely grated
- 2 garlic cloves, minced
- 1 tbsp olive oil
- 1 tbsp fresh dill, finely chopped
- Juice of half a lemon
- Salt & pepper to taste

Instructions:

- Cucumber Prep: After grating the cucumber, squeeze out as much water as possible using a cloth or sieve.
- Mix & Chill: In a bowl, combine Greek yogurt, squeezed cucumber, minced garlic, olive oil, dill, lemon juice, salt, and pepper. Mix well and refrigerate for at least an hour before serving.
- Serve & Dip: Accompany with warm pita bread for dipping.

Alternatives to Jazz it Up:

- Minty Fresh: Swap out dill for fresh mint for a zingy variant.
- Spice Kick: Add a dash of cayenne pepper for a touch of heat.

BAKLAVA PASTRY – GRECIAN GOLDEN GOODNESS

Layers of Sweetness: This rich, sweet pastry made of layers of filo filled with chopped nuts, held together by syrup and honey, is a testament to Greek dessert excellence.

Serves : 2	Prep Time : 40 Mins	Cook Time : 50 Mins

Ingredients:

- 16 sheets of filo pastry
- 200g mixed nuts (walnuts, pistachios, almonds), finely chopped
- 100g unsalted butter, melted
- 1 tsp ground cinnamon
- 200g sugar
- 250ml water
- 2 tbsp honey
- 1 slice of lemon

Instructions:

- Prep & Layer: Brush a baking dish with melted butter. Place a sheet of filo at the base, brush with more butter, and repeat until you have 8 sheets layered.
- Nutty Middle: Mix chopped nuts and cinnamon. Sprinkle half over the filo. Layer another 4 sheets of filo, brushing each with butter. Add the remaining nut mix. Finish with the last 4 filo sheets, brushing each with butter.
- Slice & Bake: Pre-cut into diamond or square shapes using a sharp knife. Bake in a preheated oven at 180°C for 35-40 minutes or until golden brown.
- Syrup Soak: While the baklava bakes, make the syrup. Boil sugar, water, honey, and a slice of lemon until sugar dissolves and the mixture is clear. Simmer for 10 minutes. Once baklava is baked, pour the hot syrup over the warm baklava.
- Rest & Relish: Allow to cool and let the syrup soak in for several hours before serving.

Alternatives to Jazz it Up:

- Orange Essence: Add a touch of orange zest or orange blossom water to the syrup for a citrusy fragrance.
- Spice It Up: A pinch of ground cloves in the nut mixture can introduce an added depth of flavor.

CHEESE FONDUE – ALPINE'S LIQUID GOLD

Dip & Delight: Melted cheese, wine, and a hint of garlic make this classic dish a social and savory experience.

🥣 Serves : 2	🍴 Prep Time : 15 Mins	🕐 Cook Time : 20 Mins

Ingredients:

- 400g Gruyère cheese, grated
- 200g Emmental cheese, grated
- 1 clove garlic, halved
- 300ml dry white wine
- 1 tsp lemon juice
- 2 tsp cornstarch
- 2 tbsp kirsch (cherry brandy)
- Freshly ground black pepper and nutmeg

Instructions:

- **Rub & Warm:** Rub the inside of a fondue pot with the cut garlic halves. Pour in the wine and lemon juice and warm gently until hot, but not boiling.
- **Melt & Mix:** Gradually add the cheese, stirring constantly until melted. In a separate bowl, mix the cornstarch with kirsch to form a smooth paste, then stir into the cheese.
- **Season & Serve:** Season with black pepper and nutmeg. Serve immediately with chunks of bread for dipping.

Alternatives to Jazz it Up:

- Herb Hint: Add some finely chopped fresh herbs like parsley or chives for a fresh twist.
- Meaty Morsels: Serve with cubes of salami or ham for added depth of flavor.

RACLETTE MELT – SWISS CHEESE SENSATION

Grilled Goodness: This traditional dish of melted cheese scraped onto diners' plates is a true mountain marvel.

Serves : 2   Prep Time : 10 Mins   Cook Time : 15 Mins

Ingredients:

- 800g Raclette cheese
- Boiled small potatoes, for serving
- Gherkins, pickled onions, cured meats for accompaniment

Instructions:

- Melt & Scrape: Traditionally, the cheese is heated either by a fireplace or a special machine, then scraped onto diners' dishes.
- Serve & Savor: Serve the melted Raclette over boiled potatoes and accompany with gherkins, pickled onions, and cured meats.

Alternatives to Jazz it Up:

- Veggie Variety: Add some grilled vegetables like bell peppers, zucchini, and mushrooms to the spread.
- Spicy Sprinkle: Offer chili flakes or spicy seasonings for those who want a kick.

RÖSTI WITH SAUSAGE – CRISPY POTATO PLEASURE

Golden & Gorgeous: This potato pancake is Switzerland's answer to hash browns, often paired with flavorful sausages.

🥣 Serves : 2	🍴 Prep Time : 20 Mins	🕐 Cook Time : 20 Mins

Ingredients:

- 500g potatoes, peeled
- 1 onion, finely chopped
- Salt and pepper to taste
- 2 tbsp butter or lard
- 4 Swiss sausages, for serving

Instructions:

- Prepare & Mix: Grate the potatoes coarsely. Mix with the chopped onion and season with salt and pepper.
- Cook & Crisp: Heat butter or lard in a pan. Add the potato mixture, pressing it down. Cook until the bottom is crispy and golden. Flip and cook the other side.
- Serve & Enjoy: Serve the Rösti hot with Swiss sausages on the side.

Alternatives to Jazz it Up:

- Cheesy Center: Add some grated cheese in the middle for a gooey surprise.
- Herby Hints: Incorporate some chopped parsley or dill for freshness.

LAMB TAGINE WITH APRICOTS – A DESERT DELIGHT

Succulent & Sweet: Tender lamb melds with the sweetness of apricots in this slow-cooked masterpiece.

Serves : 2	Prep Time : 30 Mins	Cook Time : 120 Mins

Ingredients:

- 500g lamb shoulder, cubed
- 200g dried apricots
- 2 onions, finely chopped
- 2 garlic cloves, minced
- 1 tsp ground cinnamon
- 1 tsp ground cumin
- 1 tsp ground ginger
- 2 tbsp honey
- 500ml chicken stock
- 2 tbsp almond flakes, toasted
- Fresh cilantro, for garnish

Instructions:

- Brown & Set: In a tagine or heavy-bottomed pot, brown the lamb cubes. Remove and set aside.
- Sauté & Season: In the same pot, sauté onions and garlic until translucent. Add the spices and stir until aromatic.
- Combine & Cook: Return the lamb to the pot. Add apricots, honey, and chicken stock. Cover and simmer on low for 2-3 hours, until the lamb is tender.
- Garnish & Serve: Garnish with toasted almond flakes and fresh cilantro. Serve with crusty bread or couscous.

Alternatives to Jazz it Up:

- Prune Pizzazz: Replace apricots with prunes for a different flavor profile.
- Nutty Note: Add some pistachios or walnuts for added crunch.

CHICKEN PASTILLA - FLAKY FEZ FANTASY

Crispy & Creamy: This sweet and savory pie is a marriage of shredded chicken, crunchy almonds, and phyllo pastry.

🥣 Serves : 2	✂️ Prep Time : 40 Mins	🕐 Cook Time : 50 Mins

Ingredients:

- 4 chicken thighs, cooked and shredded
- 200g blanched almonds, toasted and ground
- 1 onion, chopped
- 2 garlic cloves, minced
- 1 tsp ground cinnamon
- 2 tbsp powdered sugar
- 5 sheets phyllo dough
- Melted butter, for brushing

Instructions:

- Mix & Season: In a bowl, combine shredded chicken, ground almonds, onion, garlic, cinnamon, and powdered sugar.
- Layer & Fill: In a pie dish, layer phyllo sheets, brushing each with melted butter. Fill with the chicken mixture.
- Bake & Dust: Fold over the edges of the phyllo to enclose the filling. Brush with more butter and bake at 180°C until golden. Dust with powdered sugar and cinnamon before serving.

Alternatives to Jazz it Up:

- Fruity Flair: Add some finely chopped dried apricots or raisins to the filling.
- Nutmeg Nuance: A pinch of nutmeg can elevate the aromatic experience.

RATATOUILLE – VEGETABLE SYMPHONY

A Dish with Panache: This vegetable medley, slow-cooked in rich tomato sauce, is comfort food à la Provençal.

🍲 Serves : 2	🍴 Prep Time : 20 Mins	🕐 Cook Time : 40 Mins

Ingredients:

- 1 aubergine, sliced
- 1 zucchini, sliced
- 1 bell pepper, sliced
- 1 onion, chopped
- 3 tomatoes, diced
- 3 cloves garlic, minced
- Fresh thyme and basil
- Olive oil, salt, and pepper

Instructions:

- Veggie Vibrance: In a pan, sauté the onion and garlic in olive oil until translucent. Add bell peppers and cook until softened.
- Tomato Tenderness: Add tomatoes to the pan, followed by aubergine and zucchini. Season and sprinkle with fresh herbs. Cook covered on low heat until vegetables are tender.
- Serve & Savor: Serve hot, garnished with fresh basil.

Alternatives to Jazz it Up:

- Protein Push: Add some diced chicken or sausage for an extra hearty dish.
- Cheesy Choice: Grate some Parmesan on top for a salty kick.

FISH AND CHIPS – BRITAIN'S CRISPY CROWN JEWEL

Golden & Gourmet: Imagine the waves crashing and seagulls cawing as you indulge in this iconic dish from the English coast.

🥣 Serves : 2	🍴 Prep Time : 20 Mins	⏰ Cook Time : 25 Mins

Ingredients:

- 4 white fish fillets (like cod or haddock)
- 150g plain flour, plus extra for dusting
- 200ml cold beer
- 4 large potatoes, cut into fries
- Vegetable oil, for frying
- Salt and malt vinegar, to serve

Instructions:

- Beer Brilliance: Whisk the flour and beer into a smooth batter and let it sit for 30 minutes.
- Fry Fiesta: Deep-fry the potato strips until they're golden and crispy. Place them on a paper towel and season with salt.
- Fish in a Flash: Lightly dust the fish fillets with flour, dip them in the batter, and then fry until they're a beautiful gold.
- Classic Combo: Serve the fish and chips hot, seasoned with salt and drizzled with malt vinegar.

Alternatives to Jazz it Up:

- Herb Hint: Add some chopped fresh parsley over the chips for a burst of color and flavor.
- Pea Perfect: Pair with a side of mushy peas for the authentic English experience.

BEEF WELLINGTON – THE TUDOR'S TENDER TREAT

Elegant & Exquisite: Delight in a juicy beef fillet wrapped snugly in a mushroom mixture and encased in a golden puff pastry. A dish that would make King Henry VIII envious!

Serves : 2 **Prep Time : 40 Mins** **Cook Time : 40 Mins**

Ingredients:

- 800g beef fillet
- 250g mushrooms, finely chopped
- 2 tbsp olive oil
- 1 tbsp English mustard
- 500g puff pastry
- 1 egg, beaten
- Salt and pepper, to taste

Instructions:

- Mushroom Mastery: In a pan, sauté the finely chopped mushrooms in olive oil until they release their juices. Set aside to cool.
- Beef Brilliance: Sear the beef fillet on all sides in a hot pan. Let it cool, then brush it with English mustard.
- Wrap & Roll: Roll out the puff pastry. Place the beef in the center, top with the mushroom mixture, and wrap it all up. Seal the edges and brush with the beaten egg.
- Bake & Bask: In a preheated oven at 200°C (390°F), bake the Wellington until the pastry is golden, about 25-30 minutes.

Alternatives to Jazz it Up:

- Flavorful Filling: Add some prosciutto layers between the beef and the mushroom for an extra dimension of flavor.
- Herb Hack: Incorporate fresh thyme or rosemary into the mushroom mixture for an aromatic twist.

COTTAGE PIE – THE HEARTFELT HOMESTEAD DELIGHT

Savor the Tradition: A true heartwarming classic that brings the essence of English comfort food to your plate. Dive into layers of minced meat and creamy mashed potatoes for a culinary hug!

Serves : 2   **Prep Time : 30 Mins**   **Cook Time : 40 Mins**

Ingredients:

- 500g minced beef
- 1 onion, finely chopped
- 2 carrots, diced
- 2 cloves garlic, minced
- 2 tablespoons tomato paste
- 300ml beef stock
- 2 tablespoons Worcestershire sauce
- 1 teaspoon dried thyme (or fresh)
- 1 teaspoon dried rosemary (or fresh)
- 700g potatoes, boiled and mashed
- 50g butter
- 100ml milk
- Salt and freshly ground black pepper, to taste

Instructions:

- Begin with the Base: In a large skillet over medium heat, cook the minced beef until browned. Add onions, carrots, and garlic, and sauté until softened.
- Sauce it Up: Stir in the tomato paste, followed by the beef stock, Worcestershire sauce, thyme, and rosemary. Let it simmer until the sauce thickens and the flavors meld together. Season with salt and pepper.
- Mash Magic: In a separate bowl, mash the boiled potatoes with butter and milk until smooth and creamy. Season with salt and pepper to taste.
- Layered Love: Preheat your oven to 190°C (375°F). Pour the beef mixture into a baking dish, then layer the mashed potatoes on top. Rake a fork over the surface for a rustic look.
- Golden Goodness: Bake in the preheated oven for about 20 minutes or until the top is golden brown and slightly crispy.

Alternatives to Jazz it Up:

- Cheese Crown: Sprinkle some grated cheddar cheese on the mashed potato layer before baking for an extra gooey touch.
- Veggie Boost: Mix in some green peas or corn kernels to the beef mixture for added texture and taste.
- Herb Highlights: Add some freshly chopped parsley to the mashed potatoes for a burst of color and freshness.

STICKY TOFFEE PUDDING – A DECADENT DESSERT DELIGHT

Sweet Satisfaction: Bring the comforting warmth of English dessert right into your kitchen. This classic treat promises to satisfy your sweet tooth and cozy cravings in one bite.

🥣 Serves : 2	🍴 Prep Time : 20 Mins	🕐 Cook Time : 35 Mins

Ingredients:

- 200g pitted dates, chopped
- 250ml boiling water
- 1 tsp bicarbonate of soda
- 85g unsalted butter, softened
- 175g demerara sugar
- 2 large eggs
- 185g self-raising flour
- 200ml double cream
- 2 tbsp treacle

Instructions:

- Date Softening: In a bowl, combine the chopped dates, boiling water, and bicarbonate of soda. Let it sit for about 10 minutes, allowing the dates to soften.
- Creaming Basics: In another bowl, cream the butter and sugar until light and fluffy. Gradually beat in the eggs.
- Mix & Merge: Gently fold the flour into the butter mixture, followed by the softened dates, ensuring everything is well combined.
- Bake & Await: Pour the mixture into a greased baking dish. Bake in a preheated oven at 180°C (160°C fan/gas 4) for 30-35 minutes until risen and firm to the touch.
- Toffee Temptation: While the pudding is baking, combine the double cream and treacle in a saucepan. Heat gently until it comes to a boil, then simmer for a minute, forming a luscious toffee sauce.
- Serve & Indulge: Pour the hot toffee sauce over the baked pudding and serve immediately. Vanilla ice cream or clotted cream on the side is optional but oh-so-recommended!

Alternatives to Jazz it Up:

- Nutty Crunch: Sprinkle some chopped walnuts or pecans on top for an added crunch.
- Spice Whiff: A pinch of cinnamon or nutmeg in the batter introduces a lovely warm aroma to the pudding.
- Fruity Twist: Add some dried apricots or sultanas to the batter for an extra fruity punch.

PLOUGHMAN'S LUNCH –
A RUSTIC REPAST

Countryside Classic: This traditional English meal is more of an assembly of delicious components than a recipe. It's picnic-perfect and utterly satisfying.

🥣 Serves : 2	🍴 Prep Time : 20 Mins	🕐 Cook Time : No Cook

Ingredients:

- 2 crusty bread rolls, halved
- 100g mature Cheddar cheese, sliced
- 2 pickled onions
- 4 slices of ham or roast beef
- 2 boiled eggs, halved
- 1 apple, sliced
- Pickled gherkins or cornichons
- Ale chutney or Branston pickle
- A pint of your favorite ale or cider (optional)

Instructions:

- Assembly Art: Start with a halved crusty roll on each plate.
- Layering Love: Onto the bread, layer slices of ham or roast beef, followed by slices of Cheddar cheese.
- Pickle Parade: Add a generous dollop of ale chutney or Branston pickle to complement the cheese.
- Final Touches: Around the bread, arrange the boiled eggs, pickled onions, apple slices, and gherkins. Everything should look hearty and appetizing.
- Sip & Savour: Serve this rustic feast with a pint of ale or cider, kick back, and enjoy the simple pleasures of life.

Alternatives to Jazz it Up:

- Meat Variations: Swap the ham or roast beef for smoked salmon or roast turkey for a different flavor.
- Veggie Delight: For a vegetarian version, substitute the meat with slices of grilled halloumi or a vegetarian pâté.
- Fresh Greens: Serve with a side salad of mixed greens, cherry tomatoes, and cucumber for a refreshing touch.

SWEET AND SOUR PORK – A TANGY TREAT

East Meets Feast: Experience the symphony of sweet and sour in this classic dish that brings together crispy pork and a vibrant sauce.

Serves : 2   **Prep Time : 20 Mins**   **Cook Time : 20 Mins**

Ingredients:

- 500g pork tenderloin, cut into bite-sized pieces
- Salt and pepper, to taste
- 2 tbsp soy sauce
- 1 egg, beaten
- 120g cornstarch
- Vegetable oil, for frying
- 50g pineapple chunks
- 1 bell pepper, diced
- 3 tbsp ketchup
- 1 tbsp white vinegar
- 2 tbsp brown sugar

Instructions:

- Pork Prep: Marinate the pork pieces with salt, pepper, and soy sauce for 15 minutes.
- Batter Up: Dip each pork piece into the beaten egg, then coat with cornstarch.
- Golden Fry: In a hot wok or deep fryer, fry the pork pieces until golden and crispy. Remove and drain on paper towels.
- Sauce Symphony: In the same wok, combine ketchup, vinegar, and brown sugar. Stir until bubbly. Add in pineapple chunks and bell pepper.
- Combine & Serve: Add the fried pork back into the wok. Toss until every piece is generously coated with the sauce. Serve hot.

Alternatives to Jazz it Up:

- Seafood Switch: Use prawns or fish chunks instead of pork for a maritime twist.
- Spice Spike: Add a touch of chili sauce or red pepper flakes for a spicy kick.

PEKING DUCK PANCAKES – A BEIJING DELICACY

Royal Repast: This dish traces its origins to the imperial courts of China. Unfold a pancake and discover the rich, aromatic flavors of roasted duck complemented by sweet bean sauce.

Serves : 2   Prep Time : 60 Mins   Cook Time : 15 Mins

Ingredients:

- 1 whole duck (around 1.5kg)
- 2 tbsp honey
- 1 tbsp rice vinegar
- 2 tbsp maltose or golden syrup
- 1 tbsp soy sauce
- Hot water
- Thin Chinese pancakes
- Sliced spring onions
- Julienned cucumber
- Hoisin or sweet bean sauce

Instructions:

- Duck Prep: Clean the duck and remove any innards. Prick its skin all over.
- Marinade Marvel: Combine honey, rice vinegar, maltose, and soy sauce. Brush this mixture over the duck and let it marinate for at least 4 hours, ideally overnight.
- Roast & Rest: Roast the duck in a preheated oven at 180°C (350°F) for 90 minutes, basting occasionally. Once cooked, let it rest.
- Assembly Action: Shred the duck meat and skin. Serve on a plate alongside warm pancakes, spring onions, cucumber, and sauce.
- Roll & Relish: To eat, smear a pancake with sauce, top with duck, onions, and cucumber. Roll it up and enjoy.

Alternatives to Jazz it Up:

- Sauce Selection: Try plum sauce for a fruitier contrast with the rich duck.
- Herbal Hints: Add fresh cilantro leaves for an aromatic touch.

VEGETABLE CHOW MEIN – NOODLE NIRVANA

Stir-Fry Satisfaction: Dive into this noodle delight that perfectly balances a medley of crunchy veggies with soft, savory noodles.

Serves : 2   Prep Time : 20 Mins   Cook Time : 15 Mins

Ingredients:

- 200g chow mein noodles
- 2 tbsp vegetable oil
- 1 bell pepper, sliced
- 2 carrots, julienned
- 50g snow peas
- 2 spring onions, sliced
- 3 tbsp soy sauce
- 1 tbsp oyster sauce (or vegetarian alternative)
- 1 tsp sesame oil

Instructions:

- Noodle Know-how: Cook the noodles according to package instructions, then drain and set aside.
- Veggie Venture: In a wok or large frying pan, heat the oil and stir-fry the bell pepper, carrots, and snow peas until tender-crisp.
- Noodle Time: Add the noodles and spring onions to the wok. Drizzle over soy sauce, oyster sauce, and sesame oil. Stir well to combine.
- Serve & Savor: Dish out the chow mein onto plates, garnish with extra spring onions or sesame seeds, and enjoy.

Alternatives to Jazz it Up:

- Protein Power: Add tofu cubes or shiitake mushrooms for added substance.
- Heat Hint: Introduce a splash of chili oil or some crushed red pepper for a spicy twist.

WONTON SOUP – WHOLESOME WONTON WONDERS

Bowlful of Bliss: Dive into this comforting bowl where delicate wonton parcels swim in a fragrant broth, ensuring every sip and bite is a journey of flavors.

🥣 Serves : 2	✕ Prep Time : 30 Mins	🕐 Cook Time : 20 Mins

Ingredients:

- 20 wonton wrappers
- 100g ground pork (or shrimp)
- 1 green onion, finely chopped
- 1 tsp soy sauce
- 1/2 tsp sesame oil
- Pinch of white pepper
- 800ml chicken or vegetable broth
- Bok choy or Chinese greens of choice
- Sliced mushrooms (optional)

Instructions:

- Filling Finale: Mix the ground pork, green onion, soy sauce, sesame oil, and white pepper in a bowl.
- Wonton Wrapping: Place a small spoonful of filling in the center of each wonton wrapper. Wet the edges and fold to seal, pressing out any air bubbles.
- Brothy Base: Bring the broth to a boil in a large pot. Add the bok choy and mushrooms, if using, and cook until tender.
- Wonton Dive: Gently add the wontons to the boiling broth and let them cook until they float to the top and become translucent.
- Serve & Sip: Ladle the soup into bowls, ensuring a generous number of wontons and veggies in each. Drizzle a touch more sesame oil on top, if desired.

Alternatives to Jazz it Up:

- Seafood Spin: Replace the pork with finely chopped shrimp for a seafood twist.
- Heat Hike: Add a dash of chili oil or some sliced red chilies for a touch of spice.

EGG FRIED RICE – EVERYDAY ELEGANCE

Stir-Fry Symphony: Transform leftover rice into a flavorful feast. With golden eggs and crispy veggies, this dish is simple yet supremely satisfying.

Serves : 2   **Prep Time : 15 Mins**   **Cook Time : 15 Mins**

Ingredients:

- 3 cups cooked jasmine rice (preferably left overnight in the fridge)
- 2 tbsp vegetable oil
- 3 eggs, beaten
- 1/2 cup frozen peas and carrots, thawed
- 2 green onions, sliced
- 3 tbsp soy sauce
- 1 tsp sesame oil
- Salt and pepper, to taste

Instructions:

- Egg Excellence: In a large wok or frying pan, heat a tablespoon of oil. Pour in the beaten eggs, stirring quickly to scramble. Once cooked, set aside.
- Rice Revival: In the same wok, heat the remaining oil. Add the peas and carrots, stir-frying until tender.
- Combine & Cook: Add the rice to the wok, breaking up any clumps. Stir in the soy sauce, sesame oil, and scrambled eggs. Cook until everything is well combined and the rice is heated through.
- Garnish & Gobble: Finish with green onions, a sprinkle of salt, and pepper. Serve hot.

Alternatives to Jazz it Up:

- Meaty Moments: Throw in some diced ham, chicken, or shrimp for added protein.
- Veggie Variety: Introduce bell peppers, corn, or bean sprouts for a more colorful plate.

Thank you for joining me on this delightful culinary journey across the pages of "Campus Cravings". As we close this chapter, I hope you carry with you not just an arsenal of recipes but also cherished memories of cooking, laughter, and shared meals. May the kitchen in your dorm room or apartment be a place of discovery, comfort, and creativity.

Remember, each dish you've mastered is more than a meal; it's a testament to your resourcefulness and your adventurous spirit in the kitchen. You've taken the bold step of transforming the simple act of eating into an art form that nourishes both body and soul. So, whenever you savor a bite of your homemade creations, know that you've also sprinkled a little bit of love and a dash of personal flair into every dish.

As you continue your academic and culinary adventures, let the essence of "Campus Cravings" remind you that the best flavors of life are those you create yourself. Thank you for allowing these recipes and stories to be a part of your student life. Keep craving, keep cooking, and may your plates always be as full as your hearts.

Bon appétit and best wishes

THANK YOU

please review

on amazon

BNW

PUBLISH

**Join us on your favourite platform,
Scan the QR code on
your phone or tablet**

Printed in Great Britain
by Amazon

34804726R00075